The New Americans
Recent Immigration and American Society

Edited by
Steven J. Gold and Rubén G. Rumbaut

A Series from LFB Scholarly

Culture, Class, and Work among Arab-American Women

Jen'nan Ghazal Read

LFB Scholarly Publishing LLC
New York 2004

Library of Congress Cataloging-in-Publication Data

Read, Jen'nan Ghazal, 1972-
  Culture, class, and work among Arab-American women / Jen'nan
Ghazal Read.
    p. cm. -- (The new Americans)
Includes bibliographical references and index.
  ISBN 1-59332-006-X (alk. paper)
  1. Arab American women--Social conditions. 2. Arab American
women--Employment. 3. Women immigrants--United States--Social
conditions. 4. Women immigrants--Employment--United States. 5.
Labor supply--United States. 6. Sex role--United States. 7. Arab
Americans--Ethnic identity. 8. Arab Americans--Cultural assimilation.
I. Title. II. Series: New Americans (LFB Scholarly Publishing LLC)
  E184.A65R43 2003
  331.4'089'927073--dc22

2003023712

ISBN 1-59332-006-X

Printed on acid-free 250-year-life paper.

Manufactured in the United States of America.

Contents

v

Acknowledgements

This book represents the culmination of many years of research, and I would like to take this opportunity to thank those who supported my work. This research was made possible by grants from the Arab American Institute Foundation (AAI), the American-Arab Anti-Discrimination Committee (ADC), and the Arab Community Center for Economic and Social Services (ACCESS). I would also like to thank Helen Samhan (AAI) and John Zogby (Zogby International) for their assistance in securing the sampling frames for this project. The manuscript was greatly improved by the comments and suggestions of Susan Marshall, Norval Glenn, Bob Hummer, and Arthur Sakamoto. I am grateful to the Arab-American women who responded to the survey questionnaire and provided the data for this project. Finally, I want to thank my husband Paul Read for his encouragement and support.

CHAPTER 1
Introduction

Interest in America's newer immigrant populations has increased over the past two decades in tandem with their growing size and visibility in U.S. urban centers. Despite greater attention to the growing ethnic diversity that characterizes the United States today, some ethnic populations remain less understood. As a relatively smaller immigrant group, the economic and social adjustments of Arab Americans have received less scholarly attention than other ethnic groups. The scarcity of research on Arab Americans can be seen in the dearth of the most basic statistical data on the population (for exceptions see Zogby, 1990, 1995).

Consequently, most Americans are unaware of the diversity and complexity of this ethnic group. In the aftermath of the terrorist attacks on September 11, 2001, the term "Arab American" has evolved into a catch-all category that inaccurately groups together persons of different national origins, ethnicities, and religious affiliations, all on the basis of physical characteristics thought to reflect "Arab." In reality, Arab Americans are a heterogeneous ethnic population that shares a cultural and linguistic heritage, tracing their ancestries to eighteen

1

Arabic-speaking countries in northern Africa and western Asia (El-Badry, 1994; Read, 2002).[1] Over one-half of Arab Americans are U.S.-born, 82 percent are U.S. citizens, and contrary to popular perceptions, over two-thirds are Christian not Muslim (Read, 2004; Zogby, 2001). Moreover, compared to the U.S. adult population, Arab Americans are younger, more highly educated, have higher labor force participation rates, and earn higher incomes (U.S. Bureau of the Census, 1990b). They are more likely to be employed in managerial, professional, technical, sales or administrative fields, 73 percent compared to 58 percent of Americans.

To date, few studies have addressed this diversity, especially among women. A popular stereotype of Arab-American women portrays them as Islamic traditionalists—veiled, submissive, and secluded within the home (Shaheen, 1994; Terry, 1985). However, there are numerous reasons to believe that Arab-American women's assimilation experiences are more complicated than these images would suggest. On the one hand, Arab Americans are a relatively well-educated and prosperous ethnic group, which suggests favorable conditions for women's achievements (U.S. Bureau of the Census, 1990b). On the other, Arab cultural and religious customs reinforce traditional gender roles, especially those regarding women's responsibilities in the home and family (Haddad and Smith, 1996).

This book seeks to address some of the oversights in the literature on immigrant assimilation by examining cultural

---

[1] The Census Bureau defines Arab Americans as people who trace their ancestry to Algeria, Egypt, Libya, Morocco, Sudan, Tunisia (North Africa) and to Bahrain, Iraq, Jordan, Kuwait, Lebanon, Oman, Palestine, Qatar, Saudi Arabia, Syria, United Arab Emirates, and Yemen (western Asia).

and class influences on Arab-American women's labor force activity. Not only do Arab Americans present a new case in the literature, but they also provide an exception to predominant theories of female labor force participation and offer scholars a unique opportunity to advance theoretical knowledge on modes of immigrant adaptation. In this chapter, I describe the problem under investigation, provide a brief history on Arab-American immigration patterns, discuss Arab cultural norms on women's employment, define the research objectives, and review the organization of the book.

Statement of the Problem

Research on the economic and social adaptation of immigrants occupies a substantial area in social science literature (e.g., Foner, Rumbaut, and Gold, 2000; Portes and Rumbaut, 1996, 2001). In recent years, scholars have increasingly focused on the importance of women's labor supply for the economic adaptation of immigrants (Greenless and Saenz 1999; Kahn and Whittington, 1996; Schoeni, 1998). Beyond a marker of immigrant achievement, female labor force participation is an important measure of *women's* achievement levels because it signifies access to economic power, which is strongly correlated with gender equality at the macro level.

One of the most consistent findings in existing research is that there are significant differences in women's workforce participation, both across and within U.S. ethnic populations. For example, Hispanic women are less likely to participate in the labor force than are Anglo, Black, or Asian women, and among Hispanics, Puerto

Rican women are considerably less likely to participate in the paid labor force than are Mexicans or Cubans (Kahn and Whittington, 1996). Leading explanations for these variations highlight differences in women's human capital characteristics (e.g., education), household resources, and degree of cultural assimilation in the United States (Greenless and Saenz, 1999; Schoeni, 1998).

Existing evidence suggests that these explanations may be of limited utility for examining variations in Arab-American women's labor force activity (Haddad and Smith, 1996; Read, 2004). Nearly one-third (30%) of working-age Arab-American women hold a bachelor's degree or higher, 52 percent are native-born, 78 percent are U.S. citizens, and 91 percent are proficient in the English language, all of which indicate favorable conditions for women's labor force activity (U.S. Bureau of the Census, 1990a). As a group, however, their labor force participation rates (59.9%) are below those of most other U.S. ethnic groups of women. The rates of Arab immigrant women (45.3%) contribute to this difference, ranking among the lowest of any immigrant group. Native-born Arab-American women, in contrast, have rates resembling those of U.S.-born white women, 71.7 and 73.2 percent, respectively (U.S. Bureau of the Census, 1990a).

These data indicate that the Arab-American case provides an exception to predominant theoretical explanations of women's labor market experiences, yet no study to date has examined explicitly the economic activity of this group. The case of Arab Americans is also important because they are among the fastest growing ethnic populations in U.S. urban areas today, and similar to other U.S. ethnic groups, distinct immigration patterns have produced a diverse community whose socio-economic adaptation varies by nativity, social class, and culture (Naff, 1994; Suleiman, 1999).

Origins of Diversity: Arab-American Immigration

Arab Americans are an ethnic population that emigrated from the Middle East in two distinct waves, beginning at the end of the last century (Suleiman, 1999). Today, there are an estimated three million persons of Arab descent living in the United States, roughly equal to the size of the Native-American population.

As seen in Figure 1, the first wave of immigration began in the late nineteenth century and continued through World War I. Over ninety percent of these immigrants were Christian, and the majority of them came from Greater Syria seeking better economic opportunities for their families (Naff, 1994). Believing their immigration to be temporary, most of these early Christian immigrants devoted little effort to building ethnic communities and quickly assimilated into mainstream America (Bilge and Aswad, 1996; Suleiman and Abu-Laban, 1989).

Figure 1. Arab Immigration to the United States

	First Wave:	Second Wave:
Period:	- 1870s to WW I	- WW II to present
Size:	- 350,000 to 500,000	- 600,000 and growing
Nationality:	- Greater Syria	- Geographically diverse
Emigration:	- Economic need	- Political unrest
Social class:	- Working class	- Middle and upper classes
Religion:	- 90% Christian	- 75% Muslim
Settlement:	- Assimilationist	- Nationalistic

The second wave of immigration began after World War II and continues today (Naff, 1994:23). Unlike the first group, the second wave immigrated as exiles and refugees in response to political turmoil in the Middle East, such as the 1967 and 1973 Arab-Israeli wars and the Lebanese civil war that began in 1975 (Bozorgmehr, Der-Martirosian, and Sabagh, 1996). These newer immigrants are over ninety percent Muslim and more geographically diverse, tracing their ancestries to eighteen Arabic-speaking countries (El-Badry, 1994; Pulcini, 1993). They are also better educated and have stronger attachments to their nations of origin, arriving in the United States during an era of pan-Arab nationalism with levels of political consciousness not found in earlier immigrants (Suleiman and Abu-Laban, 1989). This second wave has significantly altered the demographic profile of Arab Americans so that today over forty percent of this group is foreign born, and Islam and Christianity are about equally represented (Zogby, 1995).

Despite this diversity, Arab Americans share a common language and are united by similar cultural values, especially those regarding gender and family relations (Bilge and Aswad, 1996). For Christian and Muslim Arabs alike, Islamic values have shaped many Arab cultural values. The family is considered the foundation of the Islamic community, and kinship ties with extended family members is customary. Islamic law (sharia) has been especially influential in setting the parameters for what constitutes proper social interaction between men and women (Haddad and Smith, 1996). Arab women are considered the cornerstone of the family and community and are prescribed accordingly to the home, with primary responsibility for socializing the children (Esposito, 1998).

Their duties include modesty, premarital virginity, childbearing, and childrearing, and their family's honor is typically contingent on whether or not they fulfill these obligations (Bilge and Aswad, 1996; Haddad and Smith, 1996). Significantly, it is these shared cultural values that offers promise in understanding variations in Arab-American women's economic activity.

Research Objectives

This research constitutes the first national study of Arab-American women and is guided by two main objectives. The central objective is to extend current models of female labor force participation to examine cultural influences on Arab-American women's work activity. The study focuses specifically on dimensions of culture that sustain patriarchal gender dynamics and promote women's familial responsibilities over their public sphere participation. The second objective is to add gender to existing research on Arab Americans and challenge stereotypes of Arab-American women as Muslim traditionalists. This requires distinguishing between the effects of Arab ethnic identity and Muslim religious affiliation, which are often conflated in studies of Arab populations.

To achieve these objectives, I use data from a mail survey that I designed and administered to a national sample of 1,500 women with Arab surnames. Most national datasets classify Arab Americans with non-Hispanic whites, which contributes to the dearth of statistical data on this group and to the popularity of studies on localized Arab-American communities (for exceptions, see El-Badry, 1994; Zogby, 1990, 1995). Although Arab ethnicity can be derived from the birth and ancestry questions on the long form of the U.S. Census, this resource, alone, is insufficient for this project because it contains no information on cultural variables, such as religious affiliation, religiosity, and ethnic identity.

This study also uses U.S. Census data and a national poll of ethnic groups to place Arab-American women in a broader context with other U.S. groups of women. Because ancestry data from the 2000 census is not currently available, the study relies on data from the 1990 census. Results of the analysis challenge assumptions about Arab-American women's family and work characteristics, highlighting key similarities and differences with white, black, Hispanic, and Asian women.

Finally, this study adds gender to existing research on Arab Americans by providing a detailed portrait of Arab-American women. For example, we currently know that compared to the U.S. adult population, Arab Americans are younger, more highly educated, have higher labor force participation rates, and earn higher incomes. However, whether these outcomes reflect Arab-American women's achievements or only Arab-American men's is previously unexamined.

Organization of the Study

This study begins by establishing the importance of female labor force participation for women's achievements, and follows with a review of explanations for variations in ethnic women's economic activity (Chapter 2). Chapter 3 reviews existing research on Arab Americans, discusses patterns of immigration and assimilation, highlights important gaps in literature on Arab-American women, and demonstrates the utility of a sociological investigation of this ethnic population. After addressing these theoretical issues, I provide a detailed explanation of the research design and methodology (end of Chapter 3). The analyses then proceed in two chapters, with each chapter dedicated to one of the research objectives specified above.

The first analysis chapter assesses the validity of stereotypes of Arab-American women by comparing them to white, black, Hispanic, and Asian women on standard social status measures, such as educational attainment, labor force participation, and individual income. In this chapter, I also provide a more detailed portrait of Arab-American women sampled, which adds gender-specificity to current research on Arab Americans. Intraethnic comparisons among Muslim and Christian respondents continue to challenge myths of Arab-American women, highlighting surprising similarities between the two groups.

The second analysis chapter focuses on the primary research objective, which is to examine cultural influences on Arab-American women's achievement levels. This section of the analysis differentiates the influences of ethnicity, nativity, religion, religiosity, and gender ideology on Arab-American women's labor force participation rates and earnings. Since the dependent variable is labor force activity, I limit analyses to a subsample of respondents who are between the ages of 18 and 65 (n=416). This research concludes by offering revised explanations for ethnic women's achievements and suggesting avenues of future research.

CHAPTER 2

Theoretical Significance of Women's Labor Force Participation

A considerable body of research over the past thirty years has addressed the historical origins and persistence of gender inequality. Male domination has characterized every known society, and evolutionary theories of gender inequality have identified many possible determinants of macrolevel variations in gender stratification. Although theories differ, most scholars agree that the relative economic power allocated to men and women is one of the most important determinants of gender inequality in any given society (e.g. Blumberg, 1984; Chafetz, 1988; Cotter et al., 1998). In other words, gender equality is greatest where there is a greater balance of economic power between men and women.

Sociologists, anthropologists, and historians concur that women's economic power is primarily determined by the division of labor between the domestic and public spheres (Blumberg, 1984; Kerber, 1988; Sanday, 1974). Women's biological ability to reproduce and the subsequent social prescription of domesticity confines them to the home and keeps them dependent on men. Conversely, men are freer to participate in and control the public sphere. This freedom accords men economic power, which facilitates acquisition of other types of power, such as political and social power (Chafetz, 1988).

Though patriarchy has characterized U.S. gender relations, women's entry into the paid labor force is arguably one of the most important events in recent history for altering the dynamics of gender inequality. Industrialization and World War II pulled massive numbers of women into the paid labor force and offered them unprecedented opportunities for economic power. Today, nearly 60 percent of all U.S. women over the age of 16 are in the paid labor force, and the economic participation rates of married women have doubled since 1960, from 32 to 62 percent (US Bureau of the Census, 1998b). More importantly, this structural shift in the composition of the labor force has been accompanied by educational opportunities for women. For the first time in U.S. history, women are able to gain financial independence from men.

There are a number of distinct processes through which labor force participation shapes women's attitudes and behaviors, and thus enhances gender equality (Manza and Brooks, 1998; Plutzer, 1988). Most significantly, women's employment encourages rejection of traditional gender roles through exposure to the idea that they can do a man's job, through greater awareness of discrimination in the workplace, and through financial independence from men (Cassidy and Warren, 1996). In recent studies, full-time working women were found to be the most supportive of gender equality, followed by part-time working women, with full-time homemakers holding the most traditional attitudes (Glass, 1992).

Research further finds that female economic activity is most liberating when coupled with educational attainment.

In the above studies, class distinctions emerged among women, with the most highly educated working women holding the most egalitarian views (Cassidy and Warren, 1996; Glass, 1992). Education is an important aspect for female workers because it not only increases their employment opportunities, but also the costs of not participating in the labor force. Educated female workers are found to have greater feminist consciousness (Wilcox and Jelen, 1991), greater power in household decision-making (Orbuch and Eyster, 1997), greater political efficacy and higher political participation rates (Manza and Brooks, 1998), and better physical and mental health (for a review see Sorensen and Verbrugge, 1987). Furthermore, education increases women's reproductive control, thereby lowering fertility rates and offering greater flexibility in the public sphere (Axinn, 1993). In general, economic activity combined with education improves women's social positions through greater power at the individual, household, and societal levels.

Structural and Cultural Explanations of Ethnic Diversity

While the benefits associated with female labor force participation are well documented, scholars have increasingly recognized that not all women benefit equally from employment (Browne, 1997; Glenn, 1992; Xu and Leffler, 1992). Minority women have historically outworked white women, but with lower levels of education, they have done so more as exploited laborers than as liberated women. Black feminist scholars have been especially attentive to these ethnic differences and have highlighted the importance of ethnicity and class in defining minority women's work experiences (Baca Zinn and Dill, 1996; Collins, 1991).

As is the case for minority men, racism has impeded the economic and educational achievement of women of color by confining the vast majority of them to the lower class. Those women who manage to improve their class positions are then faced with workplace discrimination that continues to subvert their achievements (Sokoloff, 1992). As a result, only ten percent of black women find themselves in the ten highest prestige occupations, and their earnings are lower than any ethnic group of men and higher only than Hispanic women in comparable occupations (Xu and Leffler, 1992). Largely in response to black feminist research, current scholarship has evolved towards a greater recognition of ethnic and class diversity among women, and the exclusive attention to white women's economic activity has now shifted to an examination of minority women's experiences.

Two leading explanations dominate contemporary research on ethnic variations in women's economic activity. These models have a long history in studies of ethnic inequality in the United States and have alternated in popularity over the last few decades (Frazier, 1966; Lewis, 1961; Liebow, 1967). The first explanation, called the cultural model, contends that ethnic inequality reflects differences in cultural orientations toward achievement (Lewis, 1961). Successful ethnic groups are believed to value ambition, hard work, and achievement, and its members acquire these beliefs through such cultural institutions as the family and religion. Likewise, disadvantaged minority groups are believed to possess a culture of poverty that inhibits personal achievement and fosters resignation to one's plight. For instance, the income disparity between Caribbean blacks and native-born black Americans is considered a reflection of cultural differences between the two groups (Glazer and Moynihan, 1963; for a review see Kalmijn 1996). Some scholars argue that Caribbean blacks earn substantially more than native-born blacks because their culture places more value on hard work and success (Sowell, 1981). Similarly, the educational and economic success of Asian Americans and Jewish Americans is often attributed to the transmission of cultural values that encourage ambition, education, and hard work.

As gender studies evolved, cultural explanations for ethnic inequality were used to explain ethnic variations in women's economic activity. Analogous to the argument that ethnic inequality reflects different cultural orientations toward success, some propose that variations in women's work rates reflect different cultural beliefs about appropriate gender roles. These gender role attitudes, promoted through such cultural institutions as the family and religion, may encourage or dissuade female independence (Lehrer, 1995; Orbuch and Eyster, 1997; Peek, Lowe, and Williams, 1991). According to this view, the lesser employment of Hispanic women, for instance, reflects the norms and values of a pronatalist Catholic Church and of machismo and marianismo family roles, both of which operate to enhance sex segregation. Hispanic culture is therefore considered the source of Hispanic women's oppression. Black women's higher work rates, on the other hand, are seen as a cultural holdover from norms and values that originated during slavery. Black female independence emerged as a survival mechanism, but rather than being evaluated positively, according to this cultural view, it is often considered the source of a disorganized black family that is unable to properly socialize children towards achievement (for a review see Dill, 1979).

Cultural explanations for the labor force participation of women from relatively advantaged ethnic populations are slightly more complicated. While Asian culture emphasizes achievement and success, it also reinforces traditional gender roles. These two competing effects create a paradox for Asian American women; they have the highest labor force participation rates and highest average earnings of any group of women (US Bureau of the Census 1998a), yet they maintain traditional and subordinate roles in the home (Fong, 1997:95). The effects of Jewish culture on women's achievement are similarly complicated. On the one hand, Jewish culture promotes women's achievement by encouraging their accumulation of social capital. On the other hand, Jewish culture undermines gender equality by producing gendered hierarchies (for a review see Hartman and Hartman, 1996a).

The popularity of cultural explanations has decreased, however, as empirical evidence mounts in support of structural explanations for ethnic and gender inequality (Darity, Guilkey, and Winfrey, 1996; Feagin and McKinney, 2003, Waters, 1999). In recent years, a substantial literature on blacks has developed which discredits cultural arguments that link black poverty to black culture, highlighting instead how discrimination has historically blocked black advancement. Overwhelming evidence now traces the black disadvantage to discrimination in housing and lending (e.g., Massey and Denton, 1993; Oliver and Shapiro, 1995); to discrimination in education (e.g. Hawkins, 1993); and to discrimination in employment opportunities (e.g. Darity et al., 1996). To many, the cultural argument collapses in light of recent evidence that explains the income gap between Caribbean blacks and native-born blacks solely in terms of education: Caribbean blacks have higher incomes because they have more schooling (e.g. Darity et al., 1996). Similarly, the socioeconomic success of Asian and Jewish Americans is now believed to reflect the higher educational attainment levels enjoyed by both groups (e.g. Fejgin, 1995).

In explaining ethnic variations in women's achievement, the traditional argument that cultural values either foster or inhibit women's advancement has been replaced by research that focuses on structural determinants of their achievement (Fong, 1997; Ortiz and Cooney, 1984; Stier, 1991). Structural explanations for ethnic inequality among women highlight discrimination in education and employment as a key determinant of women's economic activity (Sokoloff, 1992). In 1997, 22 percent of white women had completed "4 years of college or more" compared with only 14 percent of black women and 10 percent of Hispanic women (U.S. Bureau of the Census, 1998a). Correspondingly, the median income for full-time employed white women was $26,187, compared to $22,057 for black women and only $19,929 for Hispanic women (U.S. Bureau of the Census, 1998b). Furthermore, education is most strongly associated with Asian American and Jewish American women's income levels.

The Evolution of Ethnic and Gender Studies: Recognizing Intraethnic Diversity

The cultural and structural models constitute the basis of studies in ethnic and gender inequality in the United States and are derived primarily from research on the three major ethnic populations--whites, blacks, and Hispanics. In recent years, however, the ethnic composition of the United States has undergone dramatic shifts as changing immigration policies opened America's doors to previously banned immigrant groups (Edmonston and Passel, 1994; Portes and Rumbaut, 1996, 2001). The Immigration Act of 1965 abolished country-specific quotas and established instead preferences for family reunification and refugees. As a result, the proportion of European immigrants has sharply declined and the number of Asians and Hispanics has grown rapidly (for a review see Edmonston and Passel, 1994). These newer ethnic populations not only differ from the more culturally assimilated European populations, but they also differ among themselves, emigrating in different historical periods from diverse religious, political, and social backgrounds. For example, Asian Americans derive from at least six major groups of ethnic origin, and their assimilation experiences in the United States reflect this diversity (Yamanaka and McClelland, 1994).

Acknowledging this increased heterogeneity in U.S. ethnic populations, scholars are increasingly recognizing cultural and class diversity within ethnic groups (Dodoo, 1997; Rumbaut and Portes, 2001). This research finds significant variations within ethnic groups in their access to educational and economic resources and in their degree of assimilation to the dominant U.S. culture. These differences further vary by gender; ethnic women have unique histories of immigration that distinguish their assimilation experiences in the United States from other women and men (Cainkar, 1996; Dallafar, 1994; Stier, 1991). Some women immigrated as wives and mothers in response to the 1965 law's emphasis on family reunification, others immigrated as refugees, and a smaller number immigrated as high-skilled workers (Yamanaka and McClelland, 1994). For instance, many Filipino women immigrated as highly educated workers and are economically prosperous relative to most other female populations. Vietnamese women, on the other hand, are primarily low-skilled refugees who have limited economic opportunities beyond manual labor (Fong, 1997). In response to this growing diversity within ethnic populations, many studies in ethnic achievement now distinguish gender, social class, ethnicity, and religion as major aspects of intraethnic diversity.

The influence of social class on ethnic achievement operates in the expected direction. Both men and women with higher educational attainment levels fare better economically than do their less educated counterparts (Portes and Rumbaut, 1996; Rumbaut and Portes, 2001). For instance, more educated Asian-American women have higher labor force participation rates and higher incomes than their lesser educated peers (Stier, 1991), and the same is true for highly educated Jewish women (Hartman and Hartman, 1996b). Beyond social class, ethnic and religious variations within these broad ethnic categories further influence women's achievement levels.

The influence of ethnicity on women's achievement has two components: 1) objective ethnicity, and 2) subjective ethnic identity. The objective component, which refers to a group's ethnic category or national origin, is the standard measurement, while ethnic identity refers to their feelings toward their native culture relative to their desire for assimilation into U.S. culture (e.g. Waters, 1990). Empirical research often uses generational status as a proxy for ethnic identity, because earlier immigrants are typically more assimilated into U.S. culture than are newer arrivals. Newer immigrants, often viewing their emigration as temporary, typically leave family and friends in their homelands. The result is commonly a stronger attachment to the values and norms of their sending countries. Among the U.S. immigrant populations, ethnic identity is also reflected in involvement in ethnic community activities, consumption of ethnic media, traveling to the sending country, and socializing with same-ethnicity friends.

To many scholars, both components of ethnicity help explain variations in outcomes of ethnic women's work activity. For example, the vaunted economic success of Asian-American women varies extensively by nationality and ethnic identity. Asian-American women of all national origins have high labor force participation rates, but with higher levels of educational attainment, Japanese, Indian, and Filipino women earn substantially more than do Korean and Vietnamese women (Yamanaka and McClelland, 1994).

Selective ethnic identification further distinguishes Asian-American women's economic activity. Asian culture values education, achievement and hard work, but it also emphasizes traditional gender roles, expecting women to be good wives and mothers and to engage in employment solely to contribute to the family's economic well-being. Asian-American women who maintain strong ties with the first set of values while eschewing traditional sex-roles fare better economically than do other Asian-

American women (Fong, 1997:93). Native-born Asian-American women are more likely than the foreign born to exhibit these traits, reflecting greater degrees of assimilation to American ideals of gender egalitarianism. For instance, native-born Japanese and Chinese women are more likely to be single, have fewer children, higher levels of education, higher employment rates, and higher earnings than their foreign-born counterparts (Yamanaka and McClelland, 1994).

In addition to social class and ethnicity, religion is increasingly identified as an important determinant of women's economic achievement (Lehrer, 1995; Read, 2002). Cultural explanations of women's achievement have tended to collapse religion and ethnicity into synonymous components of culture. For example, Hispanic women's lesser employment and higher fertility rates were believed to reflect the gender-role attitudes of a pronatalist Catholic Church (for a review see Ortiz and Cooney, 1984). However, recent studies find that religion and ethnicity may constitute distinct aspects of culture than often exert contradictory influences on ethnic achievement (Hartman and Hartman, 1996b; Sabagh and Bozorgmehr, 1994).

Recent research on Jewish women illustrates this argument. Jewish culture values education and achievement, yet ethnicity cannot explain why some Jewish women choose to stay home with children (Hartman and Hartman, 1996b). Rather, Jewish religion seems more predictive of Jewish women's public sphere activity--in 1990, Orthodox women's labor force participation rates were 18 percent compared to 38 percent for other Jewish women (Wilder and Walters, 1998:433). Orthodox women also have higher fertility rates, which further limits their ability to participate in the paid labor force.

Like ethnicity, the influence of religion on women's achievement may be conceptualized as having two components: objective religious affiliation, and more subjective feelings of religiosity (Hertel and Hughes, 1987). Religious affiliation identifies membership in a particular religious subculture, while religiosity specifies the strength of association with that group. Research finds that conservative denominations are the least gender egalitarian, placing primary emphasis on women's roles as wives and mothers over their activities in the public sphere. Consequently, women who belong to conservative religious denominations often have lower employment rates and higher fertility rates than women who belong to moderate or liberal denominations (Lehrer 1995). Religiosity is even more influential than religious affiliation because frequent participation in a community of believers serves to reinforce religious beliefs. Women participating in conservative religious denominations, where issues regarding women and the family are particularly salient, are especially restricted in their public sphere participation (Hertel and Hughes, 1987:877).

Summary

The importance of female labor force participation for altering the dynamics of U.S. gender inequality is well documented. Over the past few decades, scholarship on this topic has evolved from exclusive attention to white women's economic activity towards a greater recognition of ethnic diversity among U.S. women. To this point, scholars have offered several explanations for variations in women's labor force activity, both across and within U.S. ethnic populations.

The first explanation contends that ethnic disparities in human capital account for a majority of variations in women's labor force participation (for a review see Kahn and Whittington, 1996). Education has historically been a significant predictor of women's employment, with the most highly educated women reporting the highest levels of labor force activity (Glass, 1992). Compared to other U.S. women, for example, Hispanic women have the lowest levels of educational attainment and lowest rates of paid employment, while Asian women have the highest levels of education and the highest employment rates. Research on immigrant populations frequently links foreign-born success to the positive selectivity of educated migrants and foreign-born disadvantage to lower levels of educational attainment among immigrants (e.g., Schoeni, 1998). Overall, this body of scholarship stresses that human capital is an important determinant of female labor force participation.

A second leading explanation focuses on the impact of family conditions on ethnic women's employment decisions (e.g., Greenless and Saenz, 1999). Household budgetary constraints increase the need for women's earnings, while the availability of other household income tends to decrease it (Stier and Tienda, 1992). Similarly, the presence of children in the home, especially young children, reduces women's labor force participation rates. Conversely, older children can improve women's work opportunities by assisting them with their domestic responsibilities. Family structure is especially important for immigrant women's economic activity, since the foreign-born are more likely to maintain traditional household arrangements that may include living with extended kin. Non-nuclear family members may contribute to the family's income, thereby reducing the need for female employment, or they may provide domestic support, freeing women to participate in the domestic sphere.

Receiving less empirical attention in recent years is a third explanation that underscores the importance of cultural assimilation for women's labor force activity (Lee, 1998; Yamanaka and McClelland, 1994). According to this perspective, women who have had greater exposure to U.S. cultural values have higher work rates than those who maintain ties with their sending countries, where traditional norms are more likely to favor women's domestic roles. Nativity status and duration of U.S. residence are often used as proxies for cultural assimilation because immigrants typically maintain stronger attachments to indigenous customs and weaker ties to American ideals of gender egalitarianism. There are also class distinctions among immigrant women, with the most highly educated holding the most egalitarian views (Fong, 1997; Ortiz and Cooney, 1984). Few studies, however, assess with any specificity the impact of cultural norms on ethnic women's labor force activity, in part due to limitations of existing datasets.

CHAPTER 3

The Case for Arab Americans

Available evidence suggests that Arab-American women provide an exception to hitherto accepted theories of female labor force participation. Arab-American women's human capital and family characteristics indicate favorable conditions for women's labor force activity: they are more highly educated than most groups of U.S. women, are proficient in the English language, and have fertility rates similar to those of U.S.-born white women (U.S. Bureau of the Census, 1990a). As a group, however, their labor force participation rates are below those of most other U.S. ethnic groups of women. As seen in Figure 2, Arab-American women (59.9%) are considerably less likely to participate in the labor force than are Anglo (73.2%), Black (73.1%), Asian (70.2%), or Hispanic (65.8%) women. The rates of Arab immigrant women (45.3%) contribute to this difference, ranking among the lowest of any immigrant group. U.S.-born Arab-American women, in contrast, have rates resembling those of Anglo women, 71.7 and 73.2 percent, respectively.

To date, few studies have attempted to explain these differences among Arab-American women, especially at the national level. This chapter seeks to redress this shortcoming by extending conventional (i.e., economic) models of female labor force participation to examine the effects of culture on Arab-American women's labor force activity.

Figure 2. **Labor Force Status of Working-Age Women by Race and Ethnicity[2]**

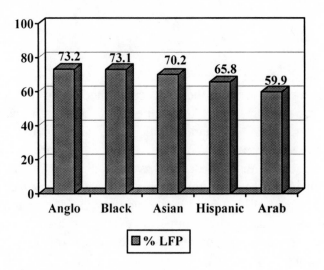

Determinants of Arab-American Women's Labor Force Activity

Although data on Arab-American women are largely missing in studies of female labor force participation, a limited number include information on Middle Eastern immigrant women, which when examined more closely, contradicts traditional findings (Bozorghmehr et al., 1996;

[2] Source: 1% Public Use Microdata Samples, 1990 U.S. Bureau of the Census, Women ages 25-64.

Schoeni, 1998). One key study that illustrates this point finds that Middle Eastern immigrant women are second only to Filipino immigrant women in their educational attainment levels and English language proficiency and equal to U.S.-born, non-Hispanic white women in their fertility rates. Their labor force participation rates, however, are among the lowest of all immigrant groups (Schoeni, 1998). As seen in Table 1, Arab immigrant women's human capital characteristics are comparable to those of Chinese and Filipino immigrant women, two groups with high rates of labor force participation.

Table 1. Comparison of Immigrant Women's Characteristics Ages 20-64[3]

	Arab	Chinese	Filipino
Labor force participation	45.9%	67.7%	85.5%
Bachelor's degree or higher	27.2	31.1	33.5
English language proficiency	84.1	67.8	95.5
U.S. resident 5 years or more	76.4	70.1	72.8
Children < 5 years in home	16.5	18.1	15.3

Analysis of U.S. Census data reveal a similar paradox *among* Arab-American women: immigrant women have lower labor force participation rates than their native-born peers (45.9% and 72.1%), and the gap remains significant after controlling for differences in their educational achievements, English language proficiency, presence of children, and age (U.S. Bureau of the Census, 1990a).

Potential explanations for this paradox exist in a more robust, qualitative literature on Arab and other Middle Eastern (e.g., Iranian) communities in the United States

---

[3] Source: U.S. Bureau of the Census, 1990.

(Aswad and Bilge, 1996; Dallafar, 1996; Haddad and Lummis, 1987). These studies emphasize the significant role that culture plays in determining the position of women of Middle Eastern descent in American society. Though Middle Eastern countries do not have a monolithic culture, they do share in common a patrilineal family structure and the belief that the family is the foundation of the community (Aswad, 1994). Women are the family's primary keeper, and their public sphere participation is discouraged in favor of their domestic responsibilities. Ultimately, women are held accountable for maintaining and reproducing Arab ethnicity in North America (Ajrouch, 1999). Coined by one scholar as "patriarchal connectivity," the term aptly describes the complex nature of relationships within Arab families, whereby women are socialized to view themselves in relation to the larger kinship structure that privileges male authority and dominance over their own achievements (Joseph, 1999).

The influence of these cultural values on Arab women's status in the Middle East is highly contentious (for a review see Esposito, 1998). To many, Arab women's lesser economic activity is indicative of their lower social positions: in 1990, Arab women made up only 13 percent of the labor force in all Arab states compared with economic activity rates of 43 percent for East Asian women and 44 percent for American women (Bozorgmehr et al., 1996:356). As seen in Table 2, there is considerable variability in women's labor force participation rates among Arab countries; however, the rates are all fairly low.

Table 2. Female Labor Force Participation by Arab Country[4]

Country	LFP (%)
Algeria	16.7
Bahrain	20.6
Egypt	22.1
Iraq	10.3
Kuwait	24.7
Lebanon	19.1
Morocco	27.1
Oman	8.6
Saudi Arabia	10.4
Tunisia	23.9

Some scholars contend that a patriarchal Arab culture limits women's work activities, especially in countries experiencing Islamic revivalism (Esposito, 1998; Toubia, 1988:10). Many Arab nations are politicizing Islam to challenge Western influences, believing that modernization has hindered rather than helped Islamic societies. Women's roles are central to this resistance; Muslim women are enjoined to fulfill their religious duties to the family and discard Western ideals of gender egalitarianism. These politicized religious reforms are believed by many to constitute the basis for Arab women's seclusion and subjugation (for a review see Esposito, 1998).

However, other scholars contend that structural conditions in the less developed Middle East are responsible for women's lesser achievement (Esposito, 1998; Hijab, 1988). Specifically, the economic stagnation in many Middle Eastern nations limits opportunities for

---

[4] Source: World Employment Report 1998-99: Employability in the Global Economy, How Training Matters, p. 218.

female education and employment. Women who are employed tend to be from the middle and upper classes and are educated abroad, which underscores the dearth of educational resources available to most women in the Middle East. Some even assert that Arab women's experiences are not too dissimilar from western women's; the latter having benefited from structural changes brought on by industrialization and two World Wars (Hijab, 1988).

While patriarchal connectivity characterizes gender relations in many parts of the Middle East, family and gender dynamics vary considerably among people of Arab descent in the United States (Esposito, 1998; Haddad and Smith, 1996). Some Arab Americans are concerned with maintaining their ethnic identity and feel that female domesticity is fundamental for preserving and reproducing Arab culture in the new world (Ajrouch, 1999; Cainkar, 1996; GhanneaBassiri, 1997; Haddad and Lummis, 1987). Others maintain pride in their Arab heritage but discard patriarchal customs perceived as inhibiting their integration and achievement in U.S. society (Haddad and Smith, 1996; Keck, 1989). These attitudes vary by social class and generational status with stronger attachments to traditional values found among the lesser educated and foreign-born (Aswad, 1994; Read, 2002, 2003). First generation immigrants are particularly committed to preserving their ethnicity, which centers largely on family stability. Immigrant women often feel more pressure than do the second- or third-generation to remain in the domestic sphere and fulfill their familial duties (e.g., Ajrouch, 1999; Haddad and Smith, 1996).

The foreign-born segment of the Arab-American population is predominantly Muslim, resulting in a conflation of religion and ethnic identity in studies of Arab communities in the United States. Muslims, however, make up only one-third of the estimated 3 million Arabs in America, with Christians comprising two-thirds of the population, reflecting distinct waves of emigration from the Middle East (Naff, 1994). While Islamic values have shaped many Arab cultural values, Muslim affiliation does not necessarily signify an Arab's attachment to cultural traditions. Many Muslim Arab Americans are secular and distinguish between religious and ethnic identity, relegating patriarchal cultural practices to Arab ethnicity (Haddad and Smith, 1996:20).

Within these broad categories of Muslim and Christian affiliation, there is considerable diversity in Arab-American women's employment patterns. Currently, we know more about Muslim Arab Americans than Christian Arab Americans, largely due to their increased visibility in the United States over the past two decades (Aswad and Bilge, 1996; GhanneaBassiri, 1997; Haddad, 1991). As is true for other immigrant groups, Muslim Arab Americans differ greatly from Muslims in their countries of origin (Haddad 1991; Walbridge 1997). Just as U.S. Catholics diverge from Italian Catholics on issues such as separation and divorce (Lehrer and Chiswick, 1993), fertility (Mosher, Williams, and Johnson, 1992), and gender role attitudes (Lehrer, 1995), Muslim Arab Americans depart from traditional Islamic customs by allowing females to attend mosques (Walbridge, 1997) and relaxing restrictions on male/female social interactions (Bilge and Aswad, 1996). For instance, many U.S. Muslims allow their daughters to attend coeducational institutions, whereas separate schools are normative in many parts of the Middle East (GhanneaBassiri, 1997; Haddad and Smith, 1996). Similarly, women frequently attend U.S. mosques, often intermingling with men during religious services, a little known practice in the Middle East (GhanneaBassiri, 1997:126; Walbridge, 1997). Within U.S. Muslim communities, women's participation in the public sphere is conditioned by myriad factors (Aswad, 1994; Walbridge, 1997). Similar to Jewish women, religiosity, ethnic identity, and social class often exert contradictory influences on Muslim women's attitudes and behaviors (c.f. Hartman and Hartman, 1996a). The influence of religiosity on women's employment operates in the expected direction: Muslim Arab-American women with stronger connections to religion usually have lower employment and higher fertility rates than women with weaker religious ties (Haddad and Smith, 1996; Read, 2003). The influence of Arab ethnic identity on women's employment is similarly restrictive, as evidenced in a study of lower-class Lebanese and Yemeni female immigrants in Dearborn, Michigan (Aswad, 1994). Women living in families with stronger ties to indigenous values and customs are less likely to be employed and have less power in major family decisions than women living in families with weaker attachments to cultural traditions. In general, cultural bonds are strongest among the most recent Arab immigrant arrivals, many of whom reside in established ethnic communities for economic, social, and psychological support (Cainkar, 1996; Suleiman, 1999). Conversely, women living in liberal Muslim families are more likely to be in the paid labor force and typically enjoy greater household decision-making power (Aswad, 1994; Read and Bartkowski, 2000).

Significantly, social class appears to have an independent effect on Muslim women's accomplishments. Even with similar levels of ethnic identity and religiosity, women with higher levels of education have higher work rates and earnings, greater personal autonomy, are more likely to share in major family decisions, and hold more egalitarian views on gender roles (Aswad, 1994; Read, 2003).

In addition to research on Arab Americans, studies of other Middle Eastern groups also underscore the importance of ethnic culture in determining immigrant women's labor supply (Bozorghmehr et al., 1996; Dallafar, 1994, 1996). Similar to women of Arab descent, Iranian women's employment rates (51.3%) fall below that of most other U.S. groups of women, despite their high educational attainment levels (39.2% hold a bachelor's degree or higher) (Bozorghmehr, 1998; U.S. Bureau of the Census, 1990a). Explanations for this seeming paradox focus on several factors related to cultural norms on gender roles: women of Iranian descent may remain out of the U.S. labor force as a family strategy to ensure that children receive proper parental attention during their upbringing; they may underreport their economic activity because they perceive their primary roles as housewife and mother; and for immigrant women, they may remain out of the labor force as a cultural carryover from practices in Iran (Bozorgmehr, 1998; Dallafar, 1994).

Hypotheses

Although there has been no systematic examination of cultural influences on women's labor force activity to date, especially at the national level, the following effects are

hypothesized for Arab-American women:
  1) immigrant women's likelihood of employment will be significantly lower than native-born women's,
  2) human capital and family characteristics will account for some, but not all, of this difference, and
  3) the effect of nativity on women's labor force activity will decrease when dimensions of ethnic and religious identity are considered.

Data and Methods

To test these hypotheses, I draw on data from the 1990 U.S. census and a national mail survey of Arab-American women. The sampling frame for the mail survey consists of the only two national lists of Arab Americans available: the Arab American Institute's membership list and a list of registered, female voters with presumed Arab surnames provided by Zogby International. Zogby International used U.S. Census Bureau information to identify twenty Metropolitan Statistical Areas (MSA) with high concentrations of Arab Americans.[5] From these twenty MSAs, Zogby derived an exhaustive list of Arab surnames from current voter registration records. The final sampling frame is representative of Arab-American regional concentration, with the five largest clusters in Los Angeles, Chicago, Detroit, New York, and Washington DC, including Virginia and Maryland suburbs (U.S. Bureau of the Census, 1990a).

---

[5] Two-thirds of Arab-Americans live in ten states: California, New York, Michigan, Florida, New Jersey, Texas, Ohio, Massachusetts, Illinois, Pennsylvania.

The survey questionnaire (Appendix A) was distributed in the spring of 2000 to a systematic, random sample of women drawn from the combined lists, after being pretested with three focus groups of Arab-American women in Washington, DC, and Austin, Texas during the fall of 1999. Because Arab surnames are common among other ethnic groups (e.g. Abraham and Moses are common among Jewish Americans) and among non-Arab Muslims (e.g. Pakistanis), I used a filter question on Arab ancestry to exclude non-Arab respondents. The question identifies the birthplace of the respondent, the respondent's mother and father, and the respondent's maternal and paternal grandparents. Since the majority of Arab-American women are U.S. citizens and 92 percent are proficient in the English language, the questionnaire was administered in English (U.S. Bureau of the Census, 1990a).

The completed sample size was 501, a response rate of 47.2 percent. The median age of women sampled is 45 and their geographic distribution is similar to that found in the 1990 census—32.4 percent are clustered in the east/northeast (mainly in the New York and Washington, DC areas), 35.3 percent are located in the midwest (mainly in Detroit and Chicago), 25.6 percent live in the west (mainly in Los Angeles), and a minority (6.7%) live in the south. Given the sampling frame characteristics, women sampled are probably older, more highly educated, and more politically involved than the Arab-American population as a whole. The most recent immigrants are likely to be under-represented in the sample, as are the most assimilated women, those who have outmarried or whose surnames have been Anglocized over time. At the same time, the sample is more nationally diverse than previous studies of this population and is more heterogeneous by religious affiliation and nativity, allowing for a more thorough examination of cultural influences on women's labor force activity.

Appendix B provides detailed information about the variables used in the analysis. Here, I briefly discuss theoretical considerations for some of the measures. The analysis focuses on three labor force outcomes, each representing an important dimension of women's economic activity. The first outcome is Arab-American women's labor force participation, the second is the degree of labor force commitment, and the third is individual earnings. Labor force participation signifies women's public sphere activity in contrast to traditional confinement within the domestic sphere, labor force commitment represents time spent in the workforce, and earnings represent their level of achievement in the labor force. These outcomes are analyzed separately because factors influencing women's entry into the labor force can have different effects on their labor force commitments and earnings (Kahn and Whittington, 1996).

To extricate cultural diversity among Arab-American women, I examine separately the influences of religious affiliation, religiosity, and ethnic identity on their labor force activity. Religious affiliation refers to membership in a particular religious subculture and is measured with a dummy variable identifying Muslim respondents.[6] Religiosity specifies the strength of religious beliefs and is measured with two variables tapping belief in scriptural inerrancy and intensity of religious beliefs over the life

---

[6] I also measure the spouse's affiliation and family's affiliation during the respondent's youth and find minimal apostasy or switching. To avoid problems of multicollinearity, only the respondent's current religious affiliation is included in the analysis.

cycle. Prior studies find that women with stronger ties to religion often have lower employment rates than women with weaker religious commitments (Hartman and Hartman, 1996b; Hertel and Hughes, 1987; Lehrer, 1995). Consequently, religiosity is expected to be even more important than religious affiliation for Arab-American women's economic activity, given the centrality of women's familial roles in both Christianity and Islam.

Ethnic identity refers to the strength of association with the Arab community, and the analysis focuses on three dimensions of Arab culture that are known to sustain patriarchal gender dynamics. The first item is homogamy, or having an Arab spouse. Homogamy indicates the importance placed on in-group solidarity and is an important mechanism for reproducing culturally normative gender expectations among Arabs and other groups, alike (c.f., Ebaugh and Chafetz, 1999; Hayani, 1999).

The second measure of Arab ethnic identity is degree of gender traditionalism. Although research finds mixed evidence for the causal order of gender ideology and women's employment (Huber and Spitze, 1981; Thornton et al., 1983), studies on U.S. immigrant populations routinely regard gender traditionalism as a measure of association with indigenous cultural norms and values (Fong, 1997; Ortiz and Cooney, 1984). This theoretical approach is especially appropriate for this study, given that gender role segregation is customary and regulated in many Arab countries in the Middle East (Esposito, 1998). Gender traditionalism is measured with a ten-item index containing questions that gauge women's support for traditional family roles, feminist issues, and non-traditional public roles (Cronbach's alpha = .734).

The final measure of ethnic identity is nativity. Prior studies suggest that ethnic identification varies by nativity, with immigrants to the United States maintaining stronger ties to indigenous cultural norms and values than the native-born (e.g., Aswad, 1994). I therefore include two variables identifying foreign-born respondents who have resided in the U.S. for "less than 15 years" and for "15 years or more," with native-born women serving as the reference group.[7]

Finally, this study includes several control variables that could reasonably affect Arab-American women's labor force participation. Household budgetary resources, household composition, and labor market region are known determinants of U.S. women's labor supply (Stier and Tienda, 1992), and are likewise important for Arab women's employment in the Middle East (Haddad, 1998). Accordingly, I consider respondent's access to household income, presence of children, presence of adult family members, and labor market region in the analysis. I also include the respondent's age to account for potential generational effects on women's labor force activity.

The analysis proceeds in two chapters. The first analysis chapter assesses the validity of stereotypes of Arab-American women by comparing them to white, black, Hispanic, and Asian women on standard social status measures, such as educational attainment, labor force participation, and individual income. In this chapter, I also provide a more detailed portrait of Arab-American women sampled, which adds gender-specificity to current research on Arab Americans. Intraethnic comparisons among

---

[7] The sample size prevented using more finite categories for duration of U.S. residence.

Muslim and Christian respondents continue to challenge myths of Arab-American women, highlighting surprising similarities between the two groups.

The second analysis chapter focuses on the primary research objective, which is to examine cultural influences on Arab-American women's achievement levels. This chapter tests the three hypotheses about immigrant women's labor force participation and provides a new framework for assessing differences in immigrant women's incorporation experiences.

CHAPTER 4

Arab-American Women in Comparative Perspective

One of the most widely held beliefs about Arab-American women is that they are veiled and secluded within the home (Bilge and Aswad, 1996; Shakir, 1997). To many, the veil symbolizes a patriarchal religious culture that universally oppresses Arab women. The purpose of this chapter is to challenge these stereotypes by comparing Arab-American women to women of other ethnic groups on standard socio-demographic measures, such as educational attainment, labor force participation, individual income, marital status, and age. This interethnic analysis challenges assumptions about Arab-American women's family and work characteristics, highlighting key similarities and differences with white, black, Hispanic, and Asian women. This chapter also adds gender to existing research on Arab Americans by providing a detailed portrait of Arab-American women sampled. Results indicate considerable intra-group diversity in women's cultural affiliations, socio-economic statuses, and family characteristics. Comparisons among foreign- and native-born and Muslim and Christian respondents underscore the complexities of this ethnic population and continue to challenge homogenous images of Arab-American women.

U.S. Census Data

To place Arab-American women in broader context with
other U.S. women, Table 3 uses U.S. Census data to
examine selected demographic characteristics for Arab-
American, white, black, Asian, and Hispanic women.[8]
Looking first at median differences in age, Arab-American
women are younger than most groups of women but share
similar life-course positions with Asian and black women
(median ages of 29.1, 31.7, and 30.5, respectively). On
family characteristics, Arab-American women look similar
to their female counterparts. Over one-half (59.2%) of the
respondents are married, which is slightly lower than
proportions of white, Asian, and Hispanic women who are
married.   Arab-American women's fertility rate is 2.07,
higher than white and Asian women (1.80 and 1.84,
respectively), but nearly equal to that of black women
(2.05) and less than Hispanic women (2.38). In contrast to
the preference for larger families in the Middle East, Arab-
American fertility rates approximate conventional U.S.
family size.

---

[8] Sources for Table 3: Current Population Surveys: Labor Force
Statistics, Work Experience of the Population; 1998, Table 2;
Population Age 16 Years and Over by Civilian Labor Force Status,
Sex, and Race and Hispanic Origin, March 1999, Table 7a; Marital
Status and Living Arrangements, March 1998, Table 1; Selected Social
Characteristics of the Population, by Region and Race, March 1998,
Table 1; Population Age 15 Years and Over by Total Money Income in
1997, Hispanic Origin and Race and Sex, March 1998, Table 11;
Selected Summary Measures of Age and Income by Hispanic Origin
and Race, March 1998, Table 1; and *National Vital Statistics Report*:
1999, Volume 48, Number 1.

Table 3. Demographic Comparison of Arab, White, Asian, Black, and Hispanic Women

	Arab	White	Asian	Black	Hispanic
Married[9]	59.2%	60.4%	61.2%	39.0%	60.3%
Fertility[10]	2.07	1.84	1.80	2.05	2.38
Education					
High school graduate+	81.1	87.2%	82.7%	77.1%	57.7%
Bachelor's degree+	28.1	24.1	38.6	15.4	10.9
Labor force participation	59.9	73.2	75.2	70.1	59.0
Median age	29.1	38.1	31.7	30.5	26.9
Sample size[11]	n=3,475	n=88,923	n=3,979	n=13,645	n=10,295

Arab-American women's educational achievements are second only to Asian women, with 28.1 percent earning a bachelor's degree or higher. This finding challenges popular stereotypes that portray Arab-American women as backwards and secluded within the home. On the other hand, their labor force participation rates are surprisingly low (59.9%), more similar to Hispanic (59%) women's than to Asian (75.2%) or white (73.2%) women's rates. Chapter 4 will examine explanations for these differences.

Table 4 continues to challenge stereotypes of Arab-American women by demonstrating the extent of heterogeneity that exists within this group. The vast majority of women are U.S.-born, with only one-third (36.1%) being born in the Middle East. Among the foreign-born, there is considerable diversity in their region of birth, with Lebanon, Egypt, Iraq, and Syria sending the

---

[9] Women "18 years +" for a better comparison with sample.

[10] Children ever born per 1000 women.

[11] Numbers in thousands except for Arab-American women.

most immigrants to the United States. Contrary to this
being a newer immigrant group, most Arab-American
women are U.S. citizens (82.1%) and an overwhelming
majority are proficient in the English language (93.3%).

Table 4: Diversity among Arab-American Women[12]

	%
Foreign-born	36.1
Country of birth	
Lebanon	26.8
Iraq	11.9
Egypt	10.4
Syria	10.0
Palestine	8.4
Jordan	7.9
Kuwait	2.0
Other[13]	22.6
U.S. citizen	82.1
English language proficiency	93.3
Sample size	n=4,520

Arab-American Survey Data

As seen in Table 5, compared to U.S. Census data, Arab-
American women sampled are older, more highly educated,
and have labor force participation rates than other groups of
U.S. women. However, these high rates of labor force

[12] U.S. Bureau of the Census, 1990, CP-3-2.
[13] Responses include Middle East, Africa, abroad, other.

participation reflect the activity of U.S.-born women of Arab descent. Similar to patterns found in U.S. Census data, immigrant women sampled have considerably lower rates of labor force activity.

Table 5: Demographic Comparison of Arab-, Jewish-, Asian-, and Italian-American Women[14]

	Read's Survey		Zogby's Culture Polls	
	Arab-American	Italian-American	Asian-American	Jewish-American
Foreign-born	48.7%	4.5%	76.6%	10.9%
Age 18-34 years	32.0	31.1	48.2	23.5
35-54 years	33.9	38.5	33.8	39.0
55 years and older	34.1	30.4	19.0	37.5
Married	62.9	68.8	68.1	66.2
Children < 17 yrs in home	33.5	31.9	36.8	28.5
Education				
High school graduate+	97.0	90.8	95.2	97.8
Bachelor's degree+	62.1	39.4	64.5	59.2
Labor Force Participation	64.3	60.0	58.3	57.1
Sample size	n=501	n=313	n=141	n=302

The achievement levels of women sampled partly reflect sampling frame characteristics: registered voters (Zogby's sampling frame) and participants in voluntary civic organizations (AAI's sampling frame) are typically older and have higher socio-economic statuses than the population as a whole (Curtis, Grabb, and Baer, 1992). Moreover, comparisons with broad census categories may accentuate Arab-American women's success by masking

---

[14] Source: Zogby International, 2000, www.zogby.com.

ethnic differences within racial groups (Yamanaka and McClelland, 1994).

For a comparison with similar U.S. *ethnic* groups, Table 5 compares the Arab-American sample to Jewish- and Asian-American women, members of relatively advantaged minority populations. Italian-American women are also included in the comparison as a baseline white ethnic group (Zogby, 2000). The subsamples of women are derived from Zogby's Culture Polls, which is a larger study of U.S. ethnic populations conducted by Zogby International between December 1999 and March 2000. Zogby applied weights to region, age, and gender to more accurately reflect the ethnic population in the United States, and the poll's margin of sampling error varied by ethnic group from +/- 4.0 percent for Italian Americans to +/- 6.3 percent for Asian Americans.

Table 5 first examines nativity differences among the groups of women. Italian- and Jewish-American women are predominantly born in the United States (95.5% and 89.1%), over half (51.3%) of Arab-American women are U.S. born, and Asian-American women are overwhelmingly foreign-born (76.6%). The respondents are evenly distributed into the three age categories (18-34 years, 35-54, 55 and older), with Asian-American women being slightly younger than the other groups. Similar to U.S. Census data reported earlier in Table 2, family characteristics are comparable. Approximately two-thirds of women are married and one-third of them have children who are less than 17 years old in the home.

Arab-American women's educational attainment levels are also comparable to these groups of women. Less than four percentage points separate Arab- and Asian-American women's college attainment levels (62.1% and 64.5%, respectively), and Jewish-American women's university credentials are similarly high at 59.2 percent. Italian-American women are the exception to these high levels, with 39.4 percent earning a bachelor's degree or more. The Arab-American sample still has higher labor force participation rates than do the other groups of women, but all groups have activity levels of around 60 percent. When compared to women from other achieving ethnic populations, such as Asian- and Jewish-Americans, Arab-American women's achievements appear more plausible.

Immigrant Selectivity and Arab-American Women's Success

Several factors related to immigrant selectivity may contribute to the extent of Arab-American women's relative success. The earliest wave of Arab emigration from the Middle East began in the late nineteenth century and continued through World War I. Like other immigrant populations who entered the United States during this period, Arab immigrants adopted an assimilationist orientation, placing a high priority on citizenship and education. Many of these working-class settlers felt that their children's education was more important than any economic contribution to the family, and consequently, by the early 1940s there was "..a marked improvement in [Arab] women's education and an increase in the number of male and female graduates from universities and professional institutions" (Suleiman, 1999:8). This community-wide emphasis on acculturation among the earlier immigrants may partly explain respondents' high achievement levels. For example, older respondents may belong to this generation, while younger respondents may be offspring of parents of this era.

At the end of World War II, a second wave of Arab immigrants began arriving in the United States. A majority of this second wave were highly educated professionals, fleeing from political unrest in various parts of the Middle East. Others began as students in American universities and extended their stay permanently, often unable to return to their countries of origin for fear of political persecution (Suleiman, 1999). Similar to U.S. Filipino and Indian female immigrants, this "brain drain" phenomenon contributes to Arab American's overall success (Yamanaka and McClelland, 1994).

Historical U.S. immigration policies have also contributed to Arab immigrant selectivity. Dating back to the late nineteenth century, U.S. immigration authorities began challenging Arabs' citizenship petitions, arguing that Arabs were of "Asiatic" descent and therefore subject to stricter regulations. Most immigrants of this earlier period came from Greater Syria[15] on the Asian continent, and their citizenship rights were denied under discriminatory statutes that limited Asian immigration. Syrians responded by tracing their ancestry to their Arab heritage, which ensured them Caucasian racial status and eligibility for U.S. citizenship. A 1915 U.S. court decision ruled that Syrians "were so closely related to Europeans that they could be considered white persons" (*Dow vs. the United States*, cited in Suleiman, 1999:7). Despite the *Dow* decision, Arab naturalization continued to be challenged until the mid-1920s, which ensured smaller flows of U.S. immigration relative to European populations.

---

[15] A geographic area that encompasses the present-day countries of Syria, Lebanon, Jordan, Israel, Palestine and parts of Iraq.

Recent U.S. legislation continues to shape Arab immigration, namely the 1996 "Illegal Immigration Reform and Immigrant Responsibility Act" and the "Anti-Terrorism and Effective Death Penalty Act." In sum, these laws target most heavily those immigrants whose origins are located in nations or regions considered a serious threat to American national security, such as the Middle East (Moore, 1999:86). Together, they limit the influx of refugees from countries with whom the United States has severed diplomatic relations, such as Iraq. Consequently, streams of newer, less-skilled immigrants in the Arab-American community remain relatively small, compared to other ethnic populations. Iraqi refugees, for example, who have less English language proficiency than earlier immigrants, make up a small proportion of the current Arab-American population. The potentially greater degree of homogeneity in Arab-American women's human capital characteristics may further explain the interethnic differences in achievements evidenced in earlier tables.

To examine the possibility that immigrant selectivity contributes to Arab-American women's achievement levels, Table 6 uses census data to compare the sample of Arab-American women to Filipino and Indian women, two Asian sub-groups that share similar immigration histories with Arab-American women (e.g. Lee, 1994). The interethnic differences in educational attainment and labor force participation found in Table 5 drastically diminish in this comparison. All three groups of women are extremely well-educated: 60.9 percent of Arab-American, 55.2 percent of Indian, and 41.6 of Filipino women have a bachelor's degree or higher. They also have high labor force participation rates, with Filipino women most likely to be employed (75.1%), Indian women least likely

(61.5%), and Arab-American women's economic activity at the midpoint (68.7%). The magnitude of Arab-American women's success seems more credible when compared to these other two high-achieving ethnic groups.

Table 6: Indicators of Immigrant Selectivity for Arab-American, Asian-Indian, and Filipino Women[16]

	Arab-American	Asian-Indian	Filipino
Educational attainment			
High school graduate or higher	97.0%	84.7%	82.6%
Bachelor's degree or higher	62.1	55.2	41.6
Labor Force Participation	64.3%	61.5%	75.1%
Sample size	n=501	n=207,657	n=492,955

Interethnic comparisons with white, black, Hispanic, and Asian women suggest that Arab-American women sampled are relatively successful and affluent. Results also demonstrate that Arab-American fertility rates are similar to other U.S. groups, which indicates more progressive family planning than is normal in traditional cultures (Haddad and Smith, 1996). In sum, these findings run counter to popular stereotypes of Arab-American women as uneducated and confined to the domestic sphere; the high achievement levels and low fertility rates of women sampled suggest they are an assimilated and nontraditional group. In the following section, I extend the analysis to provide a more detailed demographic and attitudinal profile of Arab-American women. The analysis adds gender to current research on Arab Americans and highlights greater complexity among women sampled.

---

[16] Sources: U.S. Bureau of the Census, CP-2-1, 1990, Tables 106-11; Read's survey (Arab American).

Cultural and Class Diversity

Tables 7-13 examine cultural and class diversity among a subsample of Arab-American women ages 18 to 65. Since a central variable of this study is labor force participation, subsequent analyses are limited to the 416 respondents[17] in the sample who are between the ages of 18 and 65. Compared to the full sample, these younger women are slightly more likely to be foreign-born (52.2% compared to 48.7%). Similar to the full sample, a vast majority of foreign-born women (92.6%) have lived in the United States for ten years or longer, which suggests a more assimilated group than more recent immigrant populations. Women in this subsample are also more likely to be married (67% compared to 62.7%), which reflects the presence of older women in the full sample, many of whom are widows. Over half (52.2%) of the subsample has at least one child under the age of 18 in the home (14.7% of respondents have one child, 16.3% have two, 13.0% have three, and 8.2% have four or more children in the home). Looking at the age of the children, 13 percent of respondents have one or more preschoolers in the home, 27.4 percent have one or more 5 to 13 year-olds, and 17.5 percent have at least one 14 to 17 year-old.[18] Consistent with their average age of 43 years, very few of the women in the sample have preschool children in the home, which

---

[17] I also exclude respondents who identified themselves as students or disabled.

[18] For presentation purposes, these percentages reflect the presence of children in the home, rather than the number of children in each age category (only 4% of the sample has more than one child in any one of the same age categories). In subsequent regression analyses, each age category is treated as a continuous variable, representing the actual number of children in each age group.

probably improves opportunities for their labor force activity. Studies find that preschoolers and pre-teens tend to constrain women's labor supply by adding to their domestic responsibilities, while older children often have the opposite effect, providing domestic support that frees women for paid employment (for review see Kahn and Whittington, 1996).

The influences of ethnic identity and religion on Arab-American women's public sphere activity are a central question of this study. Tables 7 and 8 examine variations among Arab-American women on these key predictor variables. Looking first at the ethnic identity measures, the respondents have extremely high levels of subjective ethnicity. When asked how they would describe their ethnicity, 41.6 percent responded with a distinctively Arab identity (e.g. "Arab" or "Lebanese"), 55 percent with a hyphenated identity (e.g. "Arab-American" or "Lebanese-American"), and only 3.4 percent identified themselves as exclusively "American." These responses suggest a more complex pattern of assimilation than revealed in earlier analyses—women can adopt U.S. family and employment patterns without losing their ethnicity.

A majority of the respondents also engage in ethnic practices on a routine basis. Fifty-six percent cook Arabic meals "frequently," 28.7 percent cook them "sometimes," and 15.2 percent "rarely" or "never" do so. Similarly, nearly three-fourths (70.3%) of the respondents speak Arabic conversationally or fluently, one-fifth (22.4%) know a few words and phrases, and 7.2 percent do not speak Arabic at all. Research on other U.S. ethnic populations finds that language and food are key elements in sustaining

Table 7: Ethnic Diversity among Arab-American Women (n=416)

Foreign-born	52.2%
U.S. resident less than 10 years	7.4
U.S. resident 10 to 20 years	20.5
U.S. resident more than 20 years	72.1
Preferred ethnic label[19]	
American	3.4%
Arab-American	55.0
Arab	41.6
Cook Arabic meals	
Never or Rarely	15.2%
Sometimes	28.7
Frequently	56.1
Arabic language fluency	
Do not speak it at all	7.2%
Know a few words and phrases	22.4
Speak it conversationally or fluently	70.3
Arab spouse (n=280)	77.1%
Arab ethnicity of five closest friends	
None of them	16.0%
1 or 2 of them	26.9
3 to 5 of them	57.1
Number of organizations shared with other Arabs	
None of them	17.7%
Some of them	38.1
Most or all of them	38.9
Follow Middle Eastern news	
Not at all or not very closely	16.9%
Somewhat closely	40.5
Very closely	42.6
Ethnicity Index[20]	21.4

---

[19] The "Arab American" category contains respondents who either identified themselves as "Arab-American" or a hyphenated American (e.g. "Lebanese-American"); the "Arab" category contains respondents who either identified themselves as "Arab" or with a specific Arab nation (e.g. "Lebanese").

[20] Mean score, index range: 8-28.

and reproducing ethnicity, and while most Arab-American women sampled maintain these ethnic practices, a smaller proportion do so to a much lesser extent or not at all (for a review, see Ebaugh and Chafetz, 2000, Chapter 6). Many of the Arab-American women's social relationships are also ethnically bound. Over half (57.1%) report that at least three of their five closest friends are of Arab ethnicity, 38.9 percent of their organizational affiliations are shared with other Arab members, and an astonishing 77.1 percent of the married respondents have an Arab spouse. These high rates of ethnic friendship and homogamy suggest that Arab Americans operate within established ethnic communities, where indigenous cultural norms and values are often maintained and reinforced. The respondents also exhibit moderate to high levels of interest in ethnic politics.[21] Forty-two percent report following Middle Eastern news "very closely," and another 40.5 percent follow it "somewhat closely." Another two-thirds of the sample claim that a presidential candidate's stance on the Middle East is "very important" in gaining their support (not shown). These eight items are compiled into an ethnic identity index ranging from 8 to 28, and the sample's mean score is relatively high at 21.4. Overall, the sample demonstrated high levels of ethnic identity.

In order to extricate cultural diversity among Arab-American women, I separate culture into its ethnic and religious components. As previous scholarship on Judeo-Christian influences has found, religion and ethnicity often constitute distinct dimensions of culture that may exert

---

[21] The sample's interest in ethnic politics likely reflects sampling frame characteristics. Zogby's sampling frame consists of registered U.S. voters, and AAI's membership list comprises persons who support Arab-American's civic and political interests.

contradictory influences on U.S. women's achievements (e.g. Hartman and Hartman, 1996a; Heaton and Cornwall, 1989). These studies consistently find that affiliation with conservative Christian and Jewish denominations, conservative religious upbringing, and religious homogamy all dampen women's labor force participation (for review see Lehrer, 1995). Religiosity is expected to be even more influential than affiliation because frequent participation in a community of believers serves to reinforce religious beliefs. Based on these prior studies, current Muslim affiliation, Muslim religious socialization, and Muslim intra-faith marriages are all expected to decrease Arab-American women's labor force participation rates.

As seen in Table 8, Arab-American women are diverse in their religious affiliations, with half (50%) reporting Christian affiliation, 44 percent Muslim, and 6 percent reporting "other" or "no" religious affiliation. A vast majority of the respondents remain members of the same faith in which they were raised: 97.6 percent of Christian and 97.2 percent of Muslim respondents reported being socialized in families of the same faith. Similarly, of married respondents, 93.6 percent of Christian and 98.5 percent of Muslim women reported having husbands of the same religious affiliation. To avoid problems of multicollinearity, only the respondent's current religious affiliation is included in the analysis.

Arab-American women also exhibit heterogeneity in the intensity of their religious beliefs. When asked to describe their own religiosity, 21 percent of the sample claimed that they were "not very" or "not at all" religious, 48.8 percent were "somewhat" religious, and 30.2 percent identified themselves as "very" religious. While a plurality of the women see themselves as moderately religious, the

remaining respondents are divided between low and high
feelings of religiosity.

Table 8: Religious Diversity among Arab-American Women (n=416)

Religious Affiliation	
Christian	50.0%
Muslim	44.0
Other or none	6.0
Respondent's religiosity	
Not at all or not very religious	21.0%
Somewhat religious	48.8
Very religious	30.2
Family's religiosity during respondent's youth	
Not at all or not very religious	20.8%
Somewhat religious	48.4
Very religious	30.8
Attends religious services	
Never	11.9%
A few times a year	36.3
Once or twice a month	17.5
Once or more a week	34.3
Reads religious materials	
Never	13.5%
A few times a year	30.6
Once or twice a month	22.2
Once or more a week	33.7
Religious conservatism	
"Holy book of my religion is literal word of God."	
Strongly disagree or disagree	21.5%
Neither agree nor disagree	21.7
Strongly agree or agree	56.8
Religiosity Index[22]	16.48

---

[22] Mean, index ranges 5-27.

Similarly, one-fifth (20.8%) described their family's religious beliefs during their youth as "not very" or "not at all religious," one-half (48.4%) felt their families were "somewhat" religious, and nearly one-third (30.4%) described their families as "very religious." The respondents continue to vary in their beliefs in scriptural inerrancy, which is a common measure of religious conservatism. A majority (56.8%) of women sampled "agreed" or "strongly agreed" that the holy book of their religion was the literal word of God, 21.7 percent neither agreed nor disagreed, and 21.5 percent reported that they "disagreed" or "strongly disagreed." In subsequent analysis, belief in scriptural literalism is expected to restrict both Christian and Muslim women's labor force activity, since the Bible and Kor'an similarly prescribe women to the home (e.g. Haddad and Smith, 1996; Sherkat, 2000).

Diversity in the sample's religiosity is further evidenced in Arab-American women's religious practices. When asked how frequently they attend religious services, 11.9 percent report "never" attending religious services, over one-third (36.3%) only do so "a few times a year," 17.5 percent attend services "once or twice a month," and one-third (34.3%) attend "once or more a week." While nearly half of the sample never or rarely attends services, the other half does so fairly regularly. This pattern is nearly identical for reading religious materials: 13.5 percent report "never" reading religious materials, 30.6 percent only read them "a few times a year," while 22.2 percent and 33.7 percent read religious materials "once or twice a month" and "once or more a week," respectively. On a religiosity index comprised of these five measures (respondent's and family's religiosity, religious reading, attendance, and fundamentalism), the sample had a mean score of 16.48 (ranging from 5 to 27). On average, the sample appears moderately religious. However, while some Arab-American women adhere strictly to their faith traditions, other respondents follow more secular patterns. With moderate to high levels of Arab ethnicity and religiosity, women sampled might be expected to hold traditional gender role beliefs. Arab cultural norms favor women's familial roles, as do Muslim and Christian tenets. Despite their cultural affiliations, however, Table 9 finds that Arab-American women sampled are fairly progressive, especially in their attitudes on traditional family roles. For example, an overwhelming majority (83.8%) said that they "disagreed" or "strongly disagreed" with the statement, "It is better for everyone if the husband makes the major decisions for the family." Another five percent were ambivalent, and 11.6 percent held more traditional views, agreeing or strongly agreeing with the statement. Similarly, 90.5 percent of respondents believed that if a husband and wife both work full-time, they should share in housework equally, with 6.1 percent dissenting (3.4% neither agreed nor disagreed).

The women sampled also support raising egalitarian children, which is surprising since the traditional Arab family defines distinct gender roles for its members. Ninety-two percent of the sample "strongly agreed" or "agreed" that parents should encourage just as much independence in their daughters as in their sons, while only 4.9 percent "strongly disagreed" or "disagreed." Respondents were least progressive in their attitudes toward mother's employment when preschool children are present in the home: 46 percent believed that children would suffer if their mothers were employed, and 36 percent disagreed (19% neither agreed nor disagreed). The high educational attainment level of this sample likely influences the magnitude of Arab-American women's nontraditional views on the family.

Table 9: Gender Role Attitudes among Arab-American Women

Better for everyone if husband makes major decisions for family

Strongly disagree or disagree	83.8%
Neither agree nor disagree	4.6
Strongly agree or agree	11.6

If husband and wife both work full-time, housework should be shared equally

Strongly agree or agree	90.5%
Neither agree nor disagree	3.4
Strongly disagree or disagree	6.1

Parents should encourage just as much independence in their daughters as in their sons

Strongly agree or agree	91.7%
Neither agree nor disagree	3.4
Strongly disagree or disagree	4.9

Preschool children will likely suffer if their mother is employed

Strongly disagree or disagree	36.0%
Neither agree nor disagree	19.0
Strongly agree or agree	46.0

Women should be allowed to lead religious services

Strongly agree or agree	58.3%
Neither agree nor disagree	19.9
Strongly disagree or disagree	21.8

Likelihood of voting for female Presidential candidate

Very likely	62.2%
Somewhat likely	26.3
Not very or not at all likely	11.6
Gender Ideology Index[23]	18.32

---

[23] Mean, index ranges 10-44.

While many respondents eschew traditional family roles, they are less supportive of women occupying non-traditional public positions. One-fifth (21.8%) felt that women should not be allowed to lead religious services, another one-fifth neither agreed nor disagreed with the idea, and 58.3 percent were in favor of women's religious leadership. Looking at their support for a female presidential candidate, 11.6 percent said they were "not very" or "not at all" likely to vote for a woman, 26.3 percent were only "somewhat likely," and 62.2 percent were "very likely." An overall assessment of the respondents' gender ideologies reveals that the women sampled are fairly nontraditional; their mean score on a ten-item gender ideology index was 18.32 (ranges from 10 to 44 with higher scores representing greater levels of gender traditionalism). The portrait of Arab-American women sampled is beginning to look more complex—women's religious and ethnic ties imply a culturally traditional group, while their gender ideologies indicate greater levels of assimilation to U.S. norms and values.

To determine if ethnicity, religiosity, and gender ideology are independent dimensions of Arab-American women's cultural affiliations, Tables 10, 11, 12 examine Pearson's correlation matrices. Table 10 examines the relationships between ethnic identity and religiosity, Table 11 looks at religiosity and gender ideology, and Table 12 examines the strength of correlations between all three constructed indices (ethnic identity, religiosity, and traditional gender ideology). First, Table 10 illustrates that some facets of ethnicity and religiosity are related but remain separate components of Arab-American women's cultural affiliations. The strongest relationships exist between the respondents' beliefs in scriptural inerrancy and their ethnic relationships and practices. This is a revealing finding; belief in scriptural inerrancy is more than a measure of religious conservatism, it symbolizes a particular worldview held by these women. Importantly, the more structural aspects of ethnicity are strongly associated with this ideological stance, such as having an Arab spouse and friends.

Table 10: Comparative Dimensions of Ethnic Identity and Religiosity, Zero-order Correlations[24]

Religiosity: Ethnic Identity:	Scriptural inerrancy	R's religiosity	Family's religiosity	Attend services	Read materials
Arab spouse	.348**	.117*	.004	.054	.100
Arab friends	.366**	.137**	.018	.088	.106*
Number of organizations shared with other Arabs	.262**	.105*	-.022	.053	.075
Arabic language fluency	.363**	.012	-.041	-.139**	-.027
Cook Arabic meals	.344**	.182**	.065	.076	.170**
Preferred ethnic label	.065	-.009	.042	.076	.000
Follow M.E. news	.034	-.041	.018	-.111*	.003
Importance of pres. candidate's stance on M.E.	.081	-.107*	-.058	-.117*	-.076

*p= < .05   **p= < .01

All other measures of ethnicity and religiosity are weaker and not significantly correlated, and Table 12 reveals that the ethnicity and religiosity indices are also weakly correlated (.165), all of which suggests that Arab-American women's ethnic identities are largely distinct from their religious beliefs.

---

[24] All items coded so that higher scores represent greater levels of ethnic identity and religiosity.

**Table 11: Comparative Dimensions of Traditional Gender Ideology
and Religiosity, Zero-order Correlations[25]**

Religiosity:	Scriptural	R's	Family's	Attend	Read
Traditional Gender Ideology:	inerrancy	religiosity	religiosity	services	materials
Family roles:					
*Better if husband makes	.311**	.264**	.071	.182**	.221**
major decisions for family					
*Preschool children suffer if					
mother employed	.295**	.160**	.043	.071	.141**
*Parents should encourage just					
as much independence in					
daughters as in sons	.250**	.124*	.054	.103*	.173**
*If a husband and wife work					
full-time, they should share					
in household tasks equally	.111*	.084	.100*	.067	.107*
Non-traditional female roles:					
*Likelihood of voting for					
female president	.279**	.246**	.121*	.211**	.249**
*Okay for women to lead					
religious services	.448**	.353**	.101*	.281**	.248**
Feminist Orientation:					
*US still needs woman's					
mvmt to bring about equality	.130*	.200*	.057	.106*	.072
*Importance of presidential					
candidate's stance on women's					
issues in gaining support	.167**	.204**	.036	.142**	.099*
*Power of men, as a group	.139**	.125*	.038	.119*	.100*
*Power of women, as a group	.182**	.086	.119*	.007	.009

*p= < .05   **p= < .01

In contrast, Table 11 finds stronger relationships between Arab-American women's religious beliefs and their gender ideologies, especially between their belief in scriptural inerrancy and their attitudes toward appropriate female roles. For example, there is a moderately strong relationship between Arab-American women's belief in

---

[25] All items coded so that higher scores represent greater levels of religiosity and gender traditionalism.

scriptural literalism and their support for allowing husbands to make the major family decisions (.311). Similarly, belief in scriptural inerrancy is strongly correlated with opposition to non-traditional public roles, such as women religious leaders (.448). Since the Bible and Kor'an both prescribe female domesticity, these findings are not surprising. While relationships between women's religious beliefs and their feminist orientations are weaker than for other dimensions of gender ideology, they demonstrate consistently positive correlations in religiosity and gender traditionalism.

Table 12: Relationships between Indices, Zero-order Correlations

	Religiosity Index	*Traditional Gender Ideology Index*
Ethnic Identity Index	.165**	.249**
Religiosity Index		.402**

**p= < .01

Table 12 further supports the finding that Arab-American women's religious beliefs are consonant with their gender ideologies (coefficient of .402). In sum, respondents with stronger religious attachments hold more traditional views on gender than do those with weaker religious ties, a finding consistent with research on Judeo-Christian women (e.g. Lehrer, 1995).

This research aims to assess the effects of education on Arab-American women's labor force activity, in addition to the impact of cultural factors listed above. We now turn to Table 13 to examine variations in Arab-American women's educational attainment levels and labor force characteristics. Surprisingly, Arab-American women's ethnic and religious ties are not in conflict with their educational achievements. This subsample of younger respondents is even more educated than the full sample; 29.6 percent have a bachelor's degree and 38.2 percent have post-graduate or professional credentials. Moreover, the intergenerational transmission of human capital does not account for this success: one-third of the respondents' fathers and nearly one-half of their mothers have less than a high school degree (33.8% and 44.3% respectively). A vast majority of the college-educated (83%) received most or all of their training in the United States, with even most foreign-born women having U.S. educational credentials (70%). Similar to the experiences of some Asian immigrant populations, the respondents' upward mobility may partly reflect their determination to achieve the "American Dream" (for review see Edmonston and Passel, 1994). When asked if they agreed or disagreed with the statement: "If you work hard enough, you can achieve anything in the U.S.," nearly three-fourths of respondents (71.1%) said they agreed or strongly agreed.

Arab-American women's labor force characteristics reflect their educational achievements. As is the case for other U.S. women, education has a positive impact on Arab-American women's work rates, occupations, and earnings. Most women sampled are employed, 31.4 percent part-time, 47.4 percent full-time, and only 21.1 percent do not participate in the paid work force. Of those employed, over two-thirds (67.2%) occupy managerial and professional positions, a much higher proportion than for any other group of U.S. women. For example, 30 percent of Filipino and 35 percent of Asian Indian women occupied the same positions in 1990, one half the proportion of the

Arab-American sample (U.S. Bureau of the Census, 1990c).

Table 13: Class Diversity among Arab-American Women (n=416)

Respondent's education

Less than college	32.2%	
College graduate	29.6	
Post-graduate or Professional degree	38.2	

Location R's college education (n=363)

Mainly or completely in U.S.	83.2%	
Mainly or completely abroad	16.8	

Parent's education

	Father	Mother
High school graduate or less	56.5%	73.3%
Some college	9.9	10.9
College graduate or more	33.6	15.8

Labor Force Participation

Not working (0 hours/week)	21.1%
Working part-time (1-39 hrs/wk)	31.4
Working full-time (40 hrs or more/wk)	47.4

Occupational Status (n=326)

Professional or Managerial	67.2%
Manufacturing or Service	5.5
Clerical or Sales	12.0
Other (e.g. self-employed; intern)	15.3

Individual Income (n=328)

Less than $24,999	26.8%
$25,000 to $44,999	33.3
$45,000 or higher	39.9

All Household Income (n=375)

Less than $40,000	15.2%
$40,000 to $59,999	14.9
$60,000 to $79,999	17.2
$80,000 or higher	52.6

Other Household Income

Less than $20,000	29.5%
$20,000 to $50,000	37.8
More than $50,000	32.7

The respondents' individual earnings are commensurate with their occupational positions. One-fourth (26.8%) of working women reported individual earnings of less than $25,000 in 1999; one-third (33.9%) earned between $25,000 and $44,999, and 39.9 percent earned $45,000 or more, again considerably more successful than other ethnic group of women (U.S. Bureau of the Census, 1990c). The sample's relative affluence is also evident at the household level; more than one-half (52.6%) of women live in households with total earnings of $80,000 or more a year, and 15.2 percent live in households with earnings of less than $40,000. We can also identify respondents' access to additional sources of income, which may moderate their labor force participation (Stier and Tienda, 1992).[26] Nearly one-third (29.5%) of the sample is relatively disadvantaged, with access to less than $20,000 in nonlabor income; over one-third (37.8%) fares better with access to $20,000 to $50,000; and one-third (32.7%) of respondents enjoy access to more than $50,000 a year in additional family income.

To this point, analyses reveal a great deal of complexity among Arab-American women sampled. On the one hand, the respondents have strong ethnic ties and are quite religious in their beliefs and practices, all of which typically suggest cultural limitations on women's public sphere activity. On the other hand, they are highly educated, professional women with above-average individual incomes, which seems paradoxical given their strong cultural affiliations. These achievement levels are even more surprising given the sample's heterogeneity in

---

[26] I constructed this variable by subtracting women's individual earnings from household earnings.

religious affiliation and nativity status—nearly one-half (44%) of respondents are Muslim and more than one-half (52.2%) are foreign-born, proportions that suggest a less culturally assimilated group. Research finds that nativity is especially salient for Asian and Hispanic women's achievements, and subsequent regression analysis finds similar results for Arab-American women (Cooney and Ortiz 1983; Kahn and Whittington 1996; Stier 1991). Consequently, results in Table 14 provide detailed analysis of cultural and class diversity among foreign- and native-born respondents, while results in Table 15 highlight selected comparisons among Muslim and Christian respondents, many of which contradict popular stereotypes of U.S. Muslim women.

The Impact of Nativity: Variations in Cultural Assimilation

Table 14 highlights key similarities and differences between the foreign- and native-born women.[27] Looking first at religious affiliation, the foreign-born are twice as likely as the native-born to be Muslim (58.6% compared to 28.1%), which follows known patterns of Arab immigration to the United States. Yet despite differences in their affiliations as Muslims or Christians, foreign- and native-born respondents are quite similar in their religious beliefs and practices. Both groups express comparable self-assessments of their religiosity, with approximately one-fifth of foreign- and native-born women identifying

---

[27] Chi-square tests illustrate significant differences in percentages, and t-tests are used to evaluate significant differences in means.

themselves as "not very" or "not at all" religious (23.1% and 18.7%, respectively), one-half reporting being "somewhat" religious (48.2% and 49.5%), and nearly one-third identifying themselves as "very" religious (28.7% and 31.8%). Similarly, foreign- and native-born women attend religious services and read religious materials at nearly the same rates. Foreign- and native-born respondents also share similar mean scores on the five-item religiosity index (16.41 and 16.55, respectively), which indicates that there are minimal differences in Arab-American women's religiosity levels by nativity.

However, an important ideological distinction emerges among foreign- and native-born respondents in their attitudes toward scriptural inerrancy, which is a common measure of religious conservatism (e.g. Sherkat, 2000). Foreign-born respondents are considerably more likely to believe that the holy book of their religion is the literal word of God, 67.3 percent compared to less than one-half (45.4%) of native-born women. Importantly, this religious stance is strongly correlated with Arab-American women's gender ideologies, especially with their support for traditional family roles (see Table 11).

Although women sampled are fairly progressive in their gender role beliefs, foreign-born women are significantly more likely than the native-born to support the male breadwinner/female homemaker family model. Sixteen percent of the foreign-born agreed that husbands should make major family decisions, compared to only 7 percent of native-born women (79.3% and 88.5% disagreed, respectively). Similarly, foreign-born respondents were twice as likely to believe that preschool children will suffer if their mother is employed (60% compared to 28.7% of the native-born).

Table 14: Nativity Differences among Arab-American Women

	FB (n=217)	NB (n=199)	X^2
Religion and Religiosity:			
Muslim Affiliation	58.6%	28.1%	42.35**
Subjective religiosity			
Not at all or not very religious	23.1%	18.7%	1.41
Somewhat religious	48.2	49.5	
Very religious	28.7	31.8	
Religiosity over the life cycle			
Low in childhood and adulthood	12.0%	8.5%	12.01
Decreased since childhood	11.1	10.6	
Increased since childhood	10.5	11.1	
High in childhood and adulthood	66.4	69.8	
Attends religious services			
Never	14.0%	9.6%	11.87
A few times a year	40.2	32.0	
Once or twice a month	15.0	20.3	
Once or more a week	30.8	38.1	
Reads religious materials			
Never	14.4%	12.6%	9.67
A few times a year	34.7	26.9	
Once or twice a month	18.1	26.7	
Once or more a week	32.8	33.8	
Religious conservatism			
"Holy book of my religion is literal word of God."			
Strongly disagree or disagree	12.1%	31.6%	32.08**
Neither agree nor disagree	20.6	23.0	
Strongly agree or agree	67.3	45.4	
Religiosity Index	16.41	16.56	-.15[28]
Selected Gender Ideology Items:			
Better for everyone if husband makes major decisions for family			
Strongly agree or agree	16.0%	7.0%	11.41*
Neither agree nor disagree	4.7	4.5	
Strongly disagree or disagree	79.3	88.5	

---

[28] T-test for difference in means.

	FB	NB	X^2
Preschool children will likely suffer if their mother is employed			
Strongly agree or agree	60.0%	28.7%	42.65**
Neither agree nor disagree	14.9	23.5	
Strongly disagree or disagree	25.1	47.8	
Parents should encourage just as much independence in their daughters as in their sons			
Strongly agree or agree	87.0%	96.0%	28.28**
Neither agree nor disagree	5.6	1.0	
Strongly disagree or disagree	7.5	2.0	
How likely would you be to vote for a female Presidential candidate, all else being equal?			
Not very or not at all likely	12.1%	11.0%	2.89
Somewhat likely	25.9	26.7	
Very likely	62.0	62.3	
How important is a Presidential candidate's position on women's issues in gaining your support?			
Not very or not at all important	10.2%	7.5%	1.38
Moderately important	29.0	32.2	
Very important	60.8	60.3	
Gender Ideology Index	19.44	17.13	2.31[a]**
Ethnicity:			
Preferred ethnic label			
American	0.9%	6.0%	10.04**
Arab-American	56.8	53.5	
Arab	45.6	37.2	
Cook Arabic meals			
Never or Rarely	5.6%	25.6%	64.51**
Sometimes	20.4	37.7	
Frequently	74.0	36.7	
Arabic language fluency			
Do not speak it at all	2.3%	12.6%	29.24**
Know a few words and phrases	0.5	46.2	
Speak it conversationally or fluently	97.2	41.2	
Arab ethnicity of five closest friends			
None of them	6.0%	26.6%	56.94**
1 or 2 of them	21.4	32.7	
3 to 5 of them	72.5	40.7	

	FB	NB	X^2
Number of organizations shared with *** ***			
other Arab members			
None of them	12.4%	26.1%	34.01**
Some of them	33.7	47.8	
Most or all of them	53.9	26.1	
Arab spouse	89.3%	55.9%	41.13**
	(n=178)	*(n=102)*	
Follow Middle Eastern news			
Not at all or not very closely	10.6%	23.6%	27.56**
Somewhat closely	35.2	46.2	
Very closely	54.2	30.2	
Ethnicity Index	23.42	18.97	4.45^a**
Social Class:			
Respondent's education			
Less than college	36.4%	27.6%	9.53**
College graduate	30.0	29.2	
Post-graduate or Professional degree	33.6	43.2	
Father's education			
Less than high school	40.7%	26.3%	10.62*
High school graduate	19.0	26.8	
Some college	8.8	11.1	
College graduate or more	31.5	35.8	
Mother's education			
Less than high school	58.4%	28.9%	37.80**
High school graduate	23.8	34.6	
Some college	7.0	15.2	
College graduate or more	10.8	21.3	
Spouse's education			
Less than college	14.8%	14.7%	10.56*
College graduate	8.0	20.6	
Post-graduate or Professional degree	77.2	64.7	
Labor Force Participation			
Not working (0 hours/week)	26.9%	14.6%	13.63**
Working part-time (1-39 hours)	33.3	29.6	
Working full-time (40+ hours)	39.8	55.8	
Occupational Status			
Professional or Managerial	64.7%	69.3%	36.65
Manufacturing or Service	7.2	4.1	
Clerical or Sales	18.3	6.4	

	FB	NB	X^2
Individual Income			
Less than $24,999	30.6%	23.2%	11.53*
$25,000 to $44,999	25.7	40.4	
$45,000 to $64,999	17.6	18.5	
$65,000 or higher	26.1	17.9	
	(n=153)	(n=173)	
Other Household Income			
Less than $20,000	24.1%	35.2%	5.52*
$20,000 to $50,000	40.3	35.2	
More than $50,000	35.6	29.6	
Labor Market Region			
West	24.4%	17.6%	7.38
Midwest	38.2	32.2	
Northeast	25.8	35.2	
South	11.6	15.0	

These findings indicate that foreign-born respondents are more conservative than are native-born women in their support for nontraditional family roles, an ideological perspective consistently found to restrict Judeo-Christian women's labor activity.

Differences in Arab-American women's feminist orientations by nativity are much less pronounced. Two-thirds of foreign- and native-born women (62% and 62.3%) reported that they would be "very likely" to vote for a female presidential candidate, with one-tenth being "not very" or "not at all" likely (12.1% of foreign-born women and 11% of the native-born). A similar proportion claimed that a presidential candidate's stance on women's issues was "very important" in gaining their support (60.8% of foreign-born women and 60.3% of native born), again with 10.2 percent and 7.5 percent reporting that it was "not very" or "not at all" important. The educational achievements of women sampled, and the political quality of the two sampling frames (registered voters and civic organization) may contribute to the degree of women's support for feminist issues.

Looking at their ethnic identifications, cultural assimilation among Arab-American women varies extensively by nativity status. First-generation women (those who are foreign-born) identify with their Arab ethnicity to a much greater extent than do the second, third, and fourth generations combined (native-born). The respondents vary least by nativity in their preferred ethnic label, with almost half of foreign-born women (45.6%) and over one-third of the native-born (37.6%) describing themselves as specifically "Arab" (versus "Arab-American" or "American"). However, in their daily practices and social relationships, foreign-born women exhibit significantly higher levels of ethnic identification than do the native-born. Three-fourths (74%) of foreign-born women cook Arabic meals "frequently" compared to one-third (36.7%) of native-born women. Moreover, one-fourth of the native-born "never" or "rarely" cook Arabic meals, compared to only five percent of foreign-born respondents. Not surprisingly, the foreign-born are more proficient in the Arabic language, with 97.2 percent speaking it fluently or conversationally, more than twice the percentage of native-born women (41.2%).

Foreign-born women's social relationships are also more ethnically tied than are native-born respondents'. Of those married, the foreign-born are considerably more likely to have an Arab husband, 89.3% compared to 55.9% of native-born women. Foreign-born women are also more likely to surround themselves with Arab friends--nearly three-fourths (72.5%) responded that "three or more" of their five closest friends are of Arab ethnicity, compared to 40.7 percent of the native-born. Moreover, native-born

women are more than four times as likely to report that
"none" of their five closest friends are of Arab ethnicity
(26.6% compared to 6% of the foreign-born). Looking at
their organizational memberships, the foreign-born are
twice as likely as the native-born to share "most or all" of
their affiliations with other Arab members (53.9%
compared to 26.1%), while native-born women are twice as
likely to share "none" of theirs (26.1% compared to 12.4%
of the foreign-born). Finally, foreign-born women are
more likely to report following Middle Eastern news "very
closely" (54.2% compared to 30.2% of the native-born),
reflecting their interest in family and friends who remain in
their homelands (e.g. Suleiman, 1999).

In general, nativity differences in Arab-American
women's ethnic identities and gender ideologies are
expected, since foreign-born women have had greater
exposure to Arab customs and are more likely to reside in
established ethnic communities than the native-born. As is
the case with other immigrant populations, many Arab
women emigrate from the Middle East with their husbands,
and once in the United States, they typically maintain
stronger kinship networks than do their native-born
counterparts. The foreign-born population often
immigrates to U.S. ethnic communities for psychological
and economic support, maintaining strong attachments to
indigenous cultural norms and values and having greater
opportunities to meet Arab friends and spousal partners
(e.g. Swanson, 1996).

Nativity also distinguishes Arab-American women in
their class positions. Although both groups are well
educated, the native-born are slightly more likely to have a
college education, 72.6 percent compared to 63.6 percent of
the foreign-born. Native-born Arab-American women are

also more likely to reach the highest level of educational attainment, with 43.2 percent holding a post-graduate or professional degree compared to 33.6 percent of the foreign-born. Disparities in educational attainment partly reflect differences in foreign- and native-born respondents' social class origins. Foreign-born women are significantly more likely to have parents with the lowest levels of educational attainment: 40.7 percent of their fathers received less than a high school education compared to 26.3 percent of native-born women's, and the gap is even greater for mother's educational attainment. Over half (58.4%) of foreign-born women have mothers with less than a high school degree, compared to less than one-third (28.9%) of native-born respondents. Of those married, minimal differences exist in spouse's educational attainment: 85.3 percent of foreign-born and native-born women have husbands with a college degree or higher, though foreign-born women are more likely to have husbands with the highest level of educational attainment (77.3% of their spouses have a post-graduate degree compared to 64.7% of native-born women's).

An important outcome of this research is labor force participation, and Table 14 finds that Arab-American women's employment characteristics vary markedly by nativity status. Foreign-born women are less likely than the native-born to participate in the paid labor force (73.1% compared to 85.4%) and are considerably less likely to work full-time (39.8% compared to 55.8%). When they are employed, however, many foreign-born respondents fare as well as their native-born counterparts. Two-thirds (64.7%) of employed foreign-born women occupy professional and managerial positions, a proportion similar to the occupational attainments of native-born women (69.3%).

On the other hand, foreign-born women are also more likely to occupy less prestigious positions: 7.2 percent work in manufacturing and service industries compared to 4.1 percent of native-born women, and 18.3 percent work in clerical and sales positions, three times the proportion of native-born women (6.4%). The greater proportion of foreign-born women in the lowest occupational categories probably reflects their lower educational attainment levels, relative to native-born women. For both groups, these are still high levels of occupational achievement.

Finally, Table 14 examines variations in Arab-American women's individual and household earnings by nativity status. Individual earnings are a fundamental indicator of women's economic achievements, and household earnings are important because they signify women's access to economic resources. Prior research finds that financial constraints increase the need for women's labor force participation, while the availability of other household income tends to decrease it (e.g. Kahn and Whittington 1996; Stier and Tienda 1992). Looking first at individual earnings, foreign-born respondents are slightly more likely than the native-born to have the lowest incomes, and they are also more likely to earn the highest. Of those employed, 30.6 percent of the foreign-born earn "less than $24,000" a year compared to 23.2 percent of the native-born, and one-fourth (26.1%) of the foreign-born report individual incomes of "$65,000 or more" compared to 17.9 percent of the native-born. Foreign-born respondents are also more likely to live in households with greater economic resources. These results likely reflect differences among foreign- and native-born respondents in their family characteristics. Foreign-born women are more likely to be married (81.1% compared to 51.8% of native-born respondents) and to have spouses with post-graduate degrees (77.2% compared to 64.7%).

One of the most important findings in Table 14 is that foreign-born women have weaker attachments to the labor force than do native-born women. Results in Table 14 also provide some clues that might explain this variation. Since there are minimal differences in social class between the two groups, education alone may be insufficient for explaining why foreign-born women work less.[29] Cultural differences between the two groups are much more pronounced. Foreign- and native-born respondents differ in their religious affiliations as Muslims and Christians and in their degree of religious conservatism, where foreign-born women are considerably more likely than the native-born to believe in scriptural inerrancy. Correspondingly, foreign-born women are more traditional in their gender ideologies, especially in their attitudes on appropriate family roles (see correlation matrices in Table 11). Taken together, these differences in religiosity and gender traditionalism may explain foreign-born women's lower work rates (for comparison see Hartman and Hartman, 1996b; Lehrer, 1995). Further, foreign-born respondents have higher levels of ethnic identity, and while some dimensions of Arab ethnicity may be less important for women's labor force participation, some aspects, such as having an Arab spouse and friends, may serve to reinforce cultural gender expectations (Ebaugh and Chafetz, 2000).

---

[29] Foreign- and native-born women are well educated, both groups share relatively disadvantaged social class backgrounds, and of those married, most have a college-educated spouse.

Challenging Myths of U.S. Muslim Women

A marked cultural difference among Arab-American women sampled is in their religious affiliations as Christians (50%) and Muslims (44%), which offers an ideal opportunity to compare the influences of Islam and Christianity on women's attitudes and behaviors. A popular stereotype of Arab-American women portrays them as Islamic traditionalists—veiled, submissive, and oppressed in the home (for review see Bilge and Aswad, 1996). These stereotypes are based largely on images of Arab women in the Middle East and are generalized arbitrarily to Arab women globally (Shakir, 1997). Muslim feminist challenges to these stereotypes maintain that Islam is no more patriarchal than Judeo-Christianity, but few studies, if any, have compared Muslim and Christian influences on women's attitudes and behaviors.

Table 15 highlights key comparisons among Muslim and Christian Arab-American respondents, beginning with differences between the two groups and ending with some surprising similarities. Looking first at nativity, Muslim respondents are more likely than Christian respondents to be foreign-born (69.1% compared to 49.1%), which follows known patterns of emigration from the Middle East. Correspondingly, Muslim respondents have higher levels of Arab ethnicity than do Christian respondents. For example, three-fourths (74.6%) of Muslim respondents reported having "3 or more" of their 5 closest friends of Arab ethnicity compared to less than half (46.1%) of Christian respondents. Similarly, over one-half (56.2%) of Muslim respondents shared "most or all" of their organizational memberships with other Arabs compared to 30.6 percent of

Table 15: Comparison of Muslim and Christian Arab-American Women

	Muslim (n=182)	Christian (n=207)	X^2
Ethnicity:			
Foreign-born	69.2%	49.1%	33.06**
Ethnicity Index	23.23	20.10	3.13[a]**
Arab ethnicity of five closest friends			
None of them	6.6%	20.9%	41.02**
1 to 2 of them	18.8	33.0	
3 to 5 of them	74.6	46.1	
Number of organizations shared			
with other Arab members			
None of them	11.8%	23.3%	25.12**
Some of them	32.0	46.1	
Most or all of them	56.2	30.6	
Arab spouse	91.3%	63.8%	29.39**
Religiosity:			
Religiosity Index	16.60	17.26	-.66[30]
Subjective religiosity			
Not at all or not very religious	19.6%	14.6%	10.13**
Somewhat religious	56.2	47.1	
Very religious	24.2	38.3	
Attend religious services			
Never	17.9%	2.4%	65.09**
A few times a year	46.4	27.1	
Once or twice a month	11.7	23.8	
Once or more a week	24.0	46.7	
Religious conservatism			
"Holy book of my religion is literal word of God."			
Strongly disagree or disagree	6.1%	27.5%	75.94**
Neither agree nor disagree	11.7	30.9	
Strongly agree or agree	82.1	41.7	

---

[30] T-test for difference in means.

	Muslim	Christian	X^2
Gender Ideology:			
Gender Ideology Index	19.02	18.34	.68[31]
How likely would you be to vote for a female			
Presidential candidate, all else being equal?			
Not very or not at all likely	13.8%	11.1%	1.26
Somewhat likely	26.0	29.5	
Very likely	60.2	59.4	
Women should be allowed to lead			
religious services.			
Strongly disagree or disagree	23.2%	23.4%	3.50
Neither agree nor disagree	20.5	21.5	
Strongly agree or agree	56.3	55.1	
Better for everyone if husband makes			
major decisions for family			
Strongly agree or agree	15.3%	9.7%	3.26
Neither agree nor disagree	4.9	4.9	
Strongly disagree or disagree	79.8	85.4	
If a husband and wife both work full-time,			
they should share in housework equally			
Strongly disagree or disagree	7.1%	5.9%	.56
Neither agree nor disagree	3.8	3.4	
Strongly agree or agree	89.1	90.7	
Parents should encourage just as much independence			
in their daughters as in their sons			
Strongly disagree or disagree	7.6%	2.5%	12.76**
Neither agree nor disagree	5.6	1.5	
Strongly agree or agree	86.8	96.0	
Preschool children will likely suffer if their			
mother is employed			
Strongly agree or agree	56.6%	38.1%	14.33**
Neither agree nor disagree	16.5	19.5	
Strongly disagree or disagree	26.9	42.4	

---

[31] T-test for difference in means.

	Muslim	Christian	X^2
Social Class:			
Respondent's education			
High school graduate or less	12.6%	12.1%	6.01
Some college	20.3	23.2	
College graduate or higher	67.1	64.7	
Labor Force Participation			
Not working (0 hours/week)	28.6%	14.6%	16.04**
Working part-time (1-39 hours)	34.1	30.6	
Working full-time (40 hours or more)	37.3	54.8	
Individual Income			
Less than $24,999	34.5%	20.4%	12.41*
$25,000 to $44,999	27.2	38.2	
$45,000 to $64,999	16.8	18.6	
$65,000 or higher	21.5	22.8	
Other Household Income			
Less than $20,000	19.5%	36.7%	14.29**
$20,000 to $50,000	40.2	37.2	
More than $50,000	40.3	26.1	

Christian respondents, and of those married, a vast majority (91.3%) of Muslim women have an Arab spouse (compared to 63.8% of Christian respondents). These differences in ethnicity are consistent with nativity patterns among Muslim and Christian respondents; foreign-born women typically maintain stronger attachments to their sending countries and have greater involvement in ethnic communities in the United States (Haddad and Smith 1996).

Variations in women's religious beliefs and practices are more complicated. In their subjective feelings of religiosity and frequency of attendance, Christian respondents are more religious than Muslim respondents; 38.3 percent of Christian women reported that they were

82   Culture, Class, and Work

"very religious" compared to 24.2 percent of Muslim
respondents, and 14.6 percent described themselves as "not
very" or "not at all" religious, compared to one-fifth
(19.6%) of Muslim women. Similarly, one-half (46.7%) of
Christian women attended religious services "once or more
a week" compared to one-fourth (24.1%) of Muslim
respondents, and only 2.4 percent reported "never"
attending services compared to almost one-fifth (17.9%) of
Muslim women. Since many U.S. Muslim communities
allow females to attend mosques, we can only speculate as
to whether Muslim respondents' lesser attendance reflects
Islamic restrictions on women's public worship or their
own lower levels of religiosity (GhanneaBassiri; Walbridge
1997). The latter explanation seems more plausible, given
Muslim women's lower score on the religiosity index
(16.60 compared to 17.26 for Christian women) and lower
levels of subjective religiosity.

In contrast, Muslim respondents appear considerably
more religious in their degree of conservatism. Compared
to their Christian counterparts, Muslim women are twice as
likely to believe in scriptural inerrancy (82.1% compared to
41.7%), which is surprising given their lower levels of
religiosity, overall. This finding may suggest that belief in
scriptural literalism is more representative of a conservative
ideological stance than a religious attitude, per se. This
hypothesis receives support in comparisons of Muslim and
Christian respondents' gender beliefs.

Astonishingly, Muslim women are only slightly more
traditional in their gender ideologies than Christian women,
and the difference is insignificant (19.02 compared to 18.34
on the gender ideology index). Muslim and Christian
respondents are equally likely to support women's
nontraditional public sphere activity. For instance, over

one-half of Muslim and Christian women responded that they would be "very likely" to vote for a female presidential candidate, all else being equal (60.2% and 59.4%, respectively). Similarly, 56.3 percent of Muslim and 55.1 percent of Christian respondents agreed that women should be allowed to lead religious services. This finding for Muslim women is surprising, given their overwhelming belief in scriptural inerrancy (i.e., the Kor'an does not allow for female clergy). Muslim and Christian women were equally nontraditional in their views on marital roles. An overwhelming majority of both groups opposed allowing husbands to make all major family decisions (79.8% of Muslim and 85.4% of Christian respondents), and both groups agreed that if husbands and wives work full-time, they should share in housework equally (89.1% and 90.7%). Again, these attitudes are discordant with literal Kor'anic interpretations, which admonish wives to obey their husbands (Abdul-Rauf 1977).

Muslim women diverged more clearly from Christian respondents in their attitudes on maternal responsibilities. Muslim respondents were less supportive of rearing egalitarian children; 7.6 percent felt that daughters should not be given as much independence as sons compared to only 2.5 percent of Christian respondents.

Even on these measures, however, both Muslim and Christian respondents are very progressive, which is especially noteworthy given popular images of Muslim women as backwards and oppressed. What these findings reveal is a more complicated relationship between religious conservatism and gender ideology—Muslim women's greater degree of conservatism is associated specifically with their having more traditional views on motherhood, but not on other traditional family roles or nontraditional public roles.

Finally, Table 15 reveals some interesting comparisons in women's social class characteristics, many of which continue to break stereotypes of U.S. Muslim women. Amazingly, Muslim and Christian respondents are equally well educated; 67.1 and 64.7 percent have a bachelor's degree or higher, respectively. These achievements clearly discredit images of Muslim women as uneducated. Looking at their labor force activity, Muslim women are less likely to participate in the labor force than Christian respondents (28.6% compared to 14.6%), and are less likely to work full-time (37.3% compared to 54.8%); these differences may be influenced by Islamic injunctions on women's public sphere activity, or they may reflect more complicated factors, such as nativity or family social class. For example, Muslim women are almost twice as likely as Christian respondents to live in affluent households (40.2% compared to 26.1% have access to $50,000 or more in additional family income) and are considerably less likely to live in economically disadvantaged homes (19.5% compared to 36.7% of Christian respondents live in home with access to less than $20,000 in additional income). Accordingly, variations in labor force activity may reflect economic motivations, as well as cultural preferences for women's employment (e.g. Cainkar, 1999).

The most important finding in Table 15 is that images of Arab-American women's subjugation are severely overstated, and images of Muslim women are particularly flawed. Compared to other U.S. religious populations, Muslim women sampled are actually more progressive in their gender ideologies! For example, recent research found that 51.2 percent of Exclusivist Protestant women supported traditional marital roles, as did 36.8 percent of Ecumenical Protestant women, 30.9 percent of Catholic women, and 22.9 percent of women reporting no religion at all (Lehrer, 1995). Compare this to 15.3 percent of Muslim and 9.7 percent of Christian Arab-American respondents who supported this family model.[32]

Portrait of an Achieving Ethnic Population

This analysis of a national sample of Arab-American women underscores their contributions to the relative affluence enjoyed by the Arab-American population. In contrast to stereotypes of Arab-American women as uneducated and isolated in the domestic sphere (e.g. Suleiman, 1999), these respondents more closely resemble the "model minority" image of Asian-American women. On educational attainment and labor force participation, Arab-American women sampled approximate the success achieved by Filipino and Asian Indian female immigrants.

Arab-American women's achievements are not completely unexpected, since Arab Americans are a relatively prosperous ethnic group. For example, according to the 1990 U.S. Census, over one-third (36.3%) of Arab Americans aged 25 and older had a bachelor's degree or higher, 37 percent were employed in professional and managerial fields, and their mean family income was $53,337, compared with the national average of $43,803

---

[32] Lehrer used responses to the question, "It is much better for everyone if the man earns the main living and the woman takes care of the home and family" (National Survey of Families and Households). Although the question is not identical to the current study's, it taps the same concept.

(U.S. Bureau of the Census, 1990c). Nevertheless, the magnitude of Arab-American women's accomplishments is somewhat surprising. Several factors related to immigrant selectivity and sampling frame characteristics contribute to the extent of this ethnic group's success.

Among Arab-American women sampled, opportunities for their economic achievements seem complicated, even paradoxical. Respondents sustain moderate to high levels of ethnicity and religiosity, and given the strong Arab and Muslim proscriptions on women's public roles, these cultural affiliations may deter their economic activity. Nearly one-half of women sampled are foreign-born, which also suggests a less culturally assimilated group. In contrast, two-thirds of respondents are college-educated, and many are progressive in their gender ideologies. What remains unclear from these summary statistics is the extent to which education and culture influence women's labor force activity.

CHAPTER 5

Determinants of Arab-American Women's Economic Achievements

Existing research suggests that variations in U.S. ethnic women's labor force activity reflect differences in their social class characteristics and degree of cultural assimilation. This chapter tests these explanations on a national sample of Arab-American women. The women sampled are especially suited to investigate these explanations: their high educational attainment levels and progressive gender beliefs indicate favorable conditions for women's labor force participation, while high proportions of foreign-born (52.2%) and Muslim women (44%) in the sample suggest a less culturally assimilated group. Diversity in their labor force participation rates and earnings provides an opportunity to differentiate cultural and class influences on women's achievements.

The goal of this chapter is to distinguish the effects of these complex characteristics on women's labor force achievements. The analysis extends economic models of female labor force participation to examine the effects of nativity, ethnic identity, religious affiliation, and religiosity on Arab-American women's economic activity. Specifically, to what extent can variations in Arab-American women's labor force activity be explained by differences in their educational attainment levels and cultural affiliations? To what degree are the effects of education and culture on labor force activity mediated by respondents' gender ideologies and nativity status? The analysis addresses these questions by focusing on three labor force characteristics, each representing an important dimension of women's economic achievements. The first outcome under investigation is degree of Arab-American women's labor force participation, and the second outcome is the degree of their labor force commitment. Labor force participation signifies women's public sphere activity in contrast to traditional confinement within the domestic sphere, and labor force commitment is important because time spent in the workforce increases job skills and improves wage prospects (Alon et al., 2001; for a review see Marini, 1989). These labor force characteristics are analyzed separately because prior research finds that factors influencing women's entry into the labor force can have different effects on their labor force commitment (Kahn and Whittington 1996). The final outcome under investigation is individual earnings, which is the key measurement of female equality with men in stratification research (Bernhardt, Morris, and Handcock, 1995; Featherman and Hauser, 1976; Kilbourne, England, and Beron, 1994; Xu and Leffler, 1992).

Ties that Bind: Ethnic Homogamy, Religiosity, and Women's Employment

Among Arab-American women sampled, one-fifth of working-age respondents are not in the labor force, and foreign-born women are considerably less likely to work than native-born women (26.9% compared to 14.6%). We next examine explanations for these labor force variations. Table 16 presents logistic regression coefficients for the effects of education and culture on Arab-American women's labor force participation, controlling for their family characteristics and age. Model 1 examines only the effects of nativity, Model 2 assesses the importance of human capital, Model 3 tests the effects of cultural assimilation, and Model 4 analyzes the effects of all variables, including the respondent's gender ideology. Nativity is included in Model 1 as a baseline measure, and changes in the coefficients across models will help explain why immigrant women have lower labor force participation rates than the native-born. Gender ideology is excluded until the final model to examine the total and net effects of education and culture on Arab-American women's labor force participation.[33]

Before we examine results in Table 16, let me explain briefly why some variables are excluded from the analyses. Since the primary outcome under investigation is women's labor force activity, I exclude several variables that could potentially create model misspecification. For example, in analysis not shown here, frequency of cooking Arabic meals significantly dampened women's labor activity; however, logic of causal order suggests that the relationship is reversed—women who work less have more time to cook. Thus, including this variable in analyses would specify incorrectly a negative influence of Arab ethnicity

---

[33] The effect of religion on women's labor force participation may reflect their support of traditional family roles (Lehrer, 1995; Sherkat, 2000). Similarly, the influence of education may reflect women's rejection of separate male and female spheres (Glass, 1992; Thornton et al., 1983).

on women's public sphere activity. Second, I exclude factors that are statistically or substantively insignificant, such as degree of marital happiness or political affiliation. Finally, I retain factors that are substantively important for women's labor force activity, such as age and number of children, regardless of their statistical significance.

Results in Model 1 indicate that foreign-born respondents, particularly more recent immigrants, are considerably less likely than native-born women to participate in the labor force, even when considering differences in educational attainment, family characteristics, and age (Model 2). Model 2 also demonstrates the importance of individual and family resources for women's employment. Respondents with a bachelor's degree are considerably more likely than their lesser-educated peers to participate in the labor force, and the likelihood is even higher for those with a post-graduate or professional degree. The presence of young children in the home constrains their labor force activity, while the presence of adult family members increases their probability of employment. The restrictive effects of parenting likely reflect a traditional negotiation of family roles, a finding that is common in research on other U.S. women (Glass, 1992; Kahn and Whittington, 1996).

Also similar to other U.S. women, family socio-economic status conditions Arab-American women's labor force activity. Women whose nonlabor earnings[34] are less than $20,000 a year are much more likely to work compared to those women with access to greater economic resources, evidence that women's labor market activity is highly responsive to economic pressures in the home (Stier

---

[34] Nonlabor earnings reflect additional family income, excluding the respondent's individual income.

Table 16: Log Odds for the Effects of Culture on Arab-American Women's LFP, Ages 20-65 (n=416)

	Model 1 b	Model 2 b	Model 3 b	Model 4 b
Nativity				
Native-born	—	—	—	—
FB, U.S. < 15 yrs	-1.345**	-1.056*	-.553	-.364
FB, U.S. ≥ 15 yrs	-.658**	-.545*	-.254	-.141
Education				
Less than bachelor's degree		—		—
Bachelor's degree		.893**		.563*
Post-graduate degree		1.383**		.889**
Cultural characteristics				
Belief in scriptural inerrancy			-.535*	-.253
High religiosity over the life cycle			-.788**	-.092
Muslim affiliation			-.027	-.434
Homogamy				
Arab spouse			-1.320**	-1.018*
Non-Arab spouse			.304	.032
Gender traditionalism index				-.069**
Background factors				
Additional family income				
Less than $20,000		1.412**	1.252**	1.348**
$20,000 to $50,000		—	—	—
More than $50,000		-1.401**	-1.395**	-1.429**
Presence of children				
Less than 5 years old		-1.316**	-1.163**	-1.374**
5 years and older		-.116	.103	.215
Presence of adult family		.824+	.923+	.901+
Labor market region				
South		—	—	—
East		.808*	1.062*	.845*
West		.568+	.741+	.612
Midwest		.166	.351	.226
Age		.144*	.162+	.098+
Age^2		-.002*	-.002+	-.001+
-2 Log Likelihood	417.817	324.593	315.953	300.404
X^2	11.485**	104.233**	112.873**	121.714**
df	2	14	17	20

+p= < .10   *p= < .05   **p= < .01

and Tienda, 1992). In contrast, more affluent respondents are much less likely to work, which may reflect an upper-class motivation for women to remain out of the labor force as a symbol of family status, a finding not unique to Arabs (Aswad, 1994; Sherkat, 2000). Aswad (1999:180) labels this the "rich peasant" attitude of some Arab men who feel that their wives' employment shames family honor.

Although educational attainment has an important impact on Arab-American women's labor force participation, it does not explain why immigrants are less likely to work than the native-born. Model 3 considers the extent to which variations in women's cultural affiliations explain this difference.[35] Specifically, Model 3 analyzes the effects of religious affiliation, religiosity, and ethnic homogamy on respondents' labor force participation. Although the religiosity index was statistically significant (not shown here), Model 3 reveals greater substantive findings by separating religiosity into its components.

Religious identity has a restrictive impact on women's employment, and the effects are strong for those who are highly religious over the life cycle and for those who believe in scriptural inerrancy. The cumulative impact of conservative religious socialization and continued religious commitment is more significant for women's behaviors than is their degree of religiosity in any one phase of the life cycle. As studies on Jewish and Christian women find, respondents who belong to a community of believers are more likely to embrace lifestyles prescribed by their faith (Hartman and Hartman, 1996a; Sherkat, 2000).

In contrast to the strong influences of religiosity, Muslim affiliation alone does not significantly constrain

---

[35] Education is excluded to examine the total effects of cultural characteristics on Arab-American women's labor force participation.

Arab-American women's labor force participation. This finding may seem surprising, given the strong Muslim proscriptions on women's public sphere activity (Abdul-Rauf, 1977). However, one plausible explanation is that many U.S. Muslims, like liberal Christians and Jews, differentiate between religion and culture, and see compatibility between Islamic gender norms and western life (Haddad and Smith, 1996; Read and Bartkowski, 2000). Studies find that within U.S. Muslim communities, women's public sphere activity varies extensively by social class, with the most highly-educated women reporting the highest levels of labor force activity (Aswad, 1994; Walbridge, 1997). Consequently, the influence of Muslim affiliation on labor force participation may be negligible among such a highly-educated sample of women. In either case, this finding challenges cultural stereotypes that depict Arab women as oppressed collectively by Islamic doctrines.

Another cultural factor that affects women's work activity is ethnic homogamy. Respondents with a spouse of Arab descent are much less likely to participate in the labor force compared to those not married, while being married to a non-Arab does not appear to significantly influence women's probability of working. Similar to cultural dynamics in other ethnic groups, endogamy preserves Arab ethnic and religious boundaries by keeping women in the home, where they are responsible for transferring Arab cultural values to future generations (for comparisons to other ethnic groups, see Ebaugh and Chafetz, 1999, 2000).

The most interesting finding in Model 3 concerns the effects of nativity. When religion and homogamy are considered, immigrant women's likelihood of participating in the labor force approach parity with those of the native-born, and the difference between the groups is no longer significant. This finding indicates that nativity's influence on labor force participation operates through women's cultural characteristics. Specifically, foreign-born women are more conservative in their religious beliefs and have stronger attachments to their ethnic identity, as evidenced by their higher rates of homogamy.

To this point, Table 16 suggests that cultural factors have important effects on Arab-American women's labor force participation. Prior research also finds that these effects may operate through women's gender ideologies. For instance, literature on Christian influences suggests that religion inhibits women's labor force participation by reinforcing traditional gender roles (Lehrer, 1995; Orbuch and Eyster, 1997; Sherkat, 2000). Accordingly, the effects of culture on labor force participation may be direct, or they may influence labor force participation indirectly through women's gender beliefs. Although research finds mixed evidence for the causal order of gender ideology and women's employment, studies on immigrant populations routinely regard gender traditionalism as a measure of association with indigenous cultural norms and values (e.g., Fong, 1997; Ortiz and Cooney, 1984). This theoretical approach is especially appropriate for this research, given that gender role differentiation and segregation is customary and regulated in many Arab countries in the Middle East (Esposito, 1998).

Model 4 begins to untangle the complicated relationships between education, culture, gender ideology, and women's labor force participation. Though education remains a significant predictor of labor force participation, its impact is weakened slightly by the inclusion of the women's gender orientations. Women's gender ideologies influence considerably their likelihood of employment, both directly and indirectly through their cultural beliefs.[36] Each increment on the gender traditionalism index decreases Arab-American women's odds of working by 6 percent i.e., odds ratios not shown). Moreover, when gender ideology is considered, the effect of nativity decreases and the impact of religiosity is reduced to statistical insignificance. These results indicate that gender traditionalism mediates cultural influences on Arab-American women's labor force participation—ethnic and religious ties restrict women's economic achievements by increasing their support for traditional gender roles. It is noteworthy that the effect of homogamy remains strong and robust, which suggests that structural aspects of culture have an independent effect on women's behaviors.

Cultural Influences on Labor Force Commitment

Table 16 demonstrates the importance of culture for Arab-American women's labor force participation but does not address variations in their labor force commitment. Cultural influences may decrease women's opportunities to enter the labor force but may be less important in shaping how much they work (for review, see Kahn and Whittington, 1996). To explore this possibility, Table 17 presents logistic regression coefficients for the effects of

---

[36] Alternate regression models found that including education in Model 3 did not change the effects of cultural characteristics on labor force participation, and education had the same effect as it did in Model 2. Accordingly, moving from Model 3 to 4, changes in the net effects of education and culture reflect the impact of gender ideology.

education and culture on women's full-time employment. This portion of the analysis is limited to a subsample of part- and full-time, year-round workers (n=328) so that differences in women's labor force commitments are not confounded with their labor force participation. In general, results are comparable to findings for respondents' labor force participation: immigrant women are less likely than the native-born to be employed full-time, and this difference is largely explained by cultural variations between the two groups.

Table 17 also reveals three distinctive cultural influences on labor force commitment. First, the results suggest that having a spouse of Arab descent is more determinative of women's labor force participation than their labor force commitment. Second, more recent immigrants remain less likely than native-born women to work full-time even when human capital and cultural characteristics are considered, which may in part reflect the influence of unmeasured factors such as discrimination in employment opportunities (Moore, 1995; Suleiman, 1999). Third, scriptural inerrancy and religiosity over the life cycle do not affect the likelihood of full-time employment. The effects seen in Table 16 indicate that religious conservatism is more strongly associated with women's entry into the labor force than with their degree of labor force commitment. Respondents who adhere to Biblical and Kor'anic scriptures and receive consistent religious socialization over the life course are more likely to remain out of the labor force altogether.

Table 17: Log Odds for the Effects of Culture on Arab-American Women's Labor Force Commitment, Ages 20-65 (n=328)

	Model 1 b	Model 2 b	Model 3 b	Model 4 b
Nativity				
Native-born	—	—	—	—
FB, U.S. resident < 15 yrs	-1.324**	-1.542**	-1.491*	-1.311*
FB, U.S. resident ≥ 15 yrs	-.355*	-.373*	-.231	-.189
Education				
Less than bachelor's degree		—		—
Bachelor's degree and higher		.523*		.658*
Cultural characteristics				
Belief in scriptural inerrancy			.222	.581
High religiosity over the life cycle			.132	.370
Muslim affiliation			-.272	-.457
Homogamy				
Arab spouse			-.064*	.188
Non-Arab spouse			.480	.656
Gender traditionalism index				-.085**
Background factors				
Additional family income				
Less than $20,000		.691**	.661**	.786**
$20,000 to $50,000		—	—	—
More than $50,000		-.816**	-.841**	-.856**
Presence of children				
Less than 5 years old		.269	.349	.151
5 years and older		-.526	-.606	-.416
Presence of adult family		.533	.420	.439
Labor market region				
South		—	—	—
East		.060	.058	.030
West		.239	.153	.180
Midwest		-.217	-.144	-.150
Age		.203*	.217*	.174*
Age^2		-.003*	-.003*	-.002*
-2 Log Likelihood	434.341	397.449	396.879	381.448
X^2	46.902**	42.050**	42.613**	57.029**
df	2	13	17	19

+p= < .10   *p= < .05   **p= < .01

This finding suggests a more complicated relationship between women's beliefs and behaviors, and one possible explanation is that family responsibilities mediate the influence of religiosity on women's labor force decisions. Highly religious women may work less because they have higher fertility rates (Mosher et al., 1992), or they may work less because they feel more responsible for balancing their public sphere activities with their roles as mothers (Sherkat, 2000).

Table 18 considers these explanations by examining relationships between religiosity and degree of labor force commitment, controlling for presence of children in the home (cross tabulations). The religiosity index is recoded into three categories representing women with lower levels of religiosity (27.8% of the sample), those with more moderate levels of religiosity (40.8%), and women with higher levels of religiosity (31.4%).

Table 18: Arab-American Women's Labor Force Participation by Religiosity and Presence of Children

	Children in home			No children in home		
Religiosity Index:	Low	Moderate	High	Low	Moderate	High
Employment:						
Not employed	13.5%	25.0%	44.4%	9.8%	12.2%	16.4%
Employed part-time	34.6	31.5	27.8	32.1	29.7	34.5
Employed full-time	51.9	43.5	27.8	57.0	58.1	49.1
N=	52	92	72	61	74	55
	100%	100%	100%	100%	100%	100%
		Gamma= -.263**			Gamma= -.128	

**p= < .01

The first section of Table 18 examines respondents with children present in the home, and finds a moderate negative relationship between women's religiosity levels and degree of labor force commitment. Among women with children, highly religious respondents are more than three times as likely to remain in the home, compared to those with the lowest levels of religiosity (44.4% compared to 13.5%). Likewise, women with the highest levels of religiosity are considerably less likely to work full-time (27.8% compared to 51.9% of women with the lowest religiosity levels). In contrast, for those respondents who have no children in the home, religiosity is relatively unimportant for their degree of labor force commitment. For example, looking only at those respondents without children, roughly half of those with low and high levels of religiosity are employed full-time (57% and 49.1%, respectively).

Table 18 also finds a relationship between presence of children and women's degree of labor force commitment, controlling for their religiosity levels. This relationship is strongest among respondents with high religiosity levels, where children significantly dampen women's labor activity. Nearly one-half (44.4%) of women with children present in the home are out of the labor force compared to 16.4 percent of women without children, and less than one-third (27.8%) of women with children work full-time, compared to 49.1 percent of women without those domestic responsibilities.

Table 18 shows no relationship between women's religiosity levels and presence of children. Looking at the absolute numbers in the marginals, nearly one-half (46%) of women with low religiosity levels have children present in the home compared to 55 percent of those with moderate levels and 56 percent of those with high levels of religiosity. Table 18 suggests that presence of children in the home mediates the influence of religiosity on women's work commitments.

Finally, prior studies suggest that the benefits of educational attainment differ for foreign- and native-born women (Schoeni, 1998; Kahn and Whittington, 1996), and Table 19 examines this possibility among women sampled (i.e., by including interaction terms). The first column displays results for women's labor force participation, and the second column examines their labor force commitment. Expanded models in Table 19 show that the effects of education on Arab-American women's labor force activity are only significant for the foreign-born. Not unlike findings for other immigrant groups, foreign-born women may feel greater need to use their credentials for employment opportunities. The source of the respondent's college credentials (U.S. or abroad) did not change this effect and is therefore excluded from the analysis.

Table 19: Log Odds for the Interaction Effects of Education and Nativity Arab-American Women's Labor Force Activity, Ages 20-65[37]

	Labor Force Participation (n=414)	Full-time Participation (n=328)
	b	b
Foreign-born	-1.137*	-1.044*
Education		
Bachelor's degree or higher	.247	.055
Interaction		
Foreign-born*bachelor's degree+	1.521**	1.069*
-2 Log Likelihood	297.453	386.006
X^2	124.665**	54.306**

+p= < .10   *p= < .05   **p= < .01

---

[37] Models include all cultural and background factors seen in Tables 16 and 17.

Gender Traditionalism's Cultural Underpinnings

The utility of gender traditionalism for specifying the relationship between women's cultural affiliations and their labor force activity raises interesting questions regarding the process of assimilation among Arab-American women. For example, foreign-born women are more gender traditional than native-born women, and this difference largely explains why foreign-born women work less. Given the importance of gender traditionalism, to what extent do immigrant women's gender ideologies vary with length of residence in the United States? Assimilation theory proposes that acculturation is a linear process that increases with duration of U.S. residence; thus we might expect newer arrivals to be less progressive in their gender beliefs than those immigrants who have had greater exposure to U.S. norms and values (for reviews see Alba and Nee, 1997; Edmonston and Passel, 1994).[38]

To identify factors that contribute to greater levels of gender traditionalism among Arab-American women sampled, Table 20 examines ordinary least squares coefficients for the regression of gender ideology on women's cultural affiliations and educational attainments (positive coefficients reflect increases in gender traditionalism, and negative coefficients reflect decreases). The regression models also consider several family characteristics that could reasonably influence these relationships. Model 1 examines the effects of duration of U.S. residence on respondents' degree of gender

---

[38] Nativity status is more significant than length of U.S. residence for respondents' labor force participation and was excluded from the labor force analysis due to sample size constraints.

traditionalism, controlling for family structure. Results in Model 1 show that foreign-born women are more

Table 20: OLS Coefficients for Arab-American Women's Beliefs in Gender Traditionalism, Ages 20-65 (n=416)

	Model 1 b	Model 2 b	Model 3 b	Model 4 b
Education				
Bachelor's degree		-1.712**		-.365
Post-graduate degree		-3.614**		-2.036**
Cultural Characteristics				
Nativity				
Native-born	—	—	—	—
F.B., U.S. resident < 20 yrs	2.488**	2.632**	1.952**	2.101**
F.B., U.S. resident > 20 yrs	1.314**	1.056*	1.059*	.948*
Arab spouse			1.642**	1.475**
Ethnic organizations			.748+	.602
Muslim			-.570	-.418
Belief in scriptural inerrancy			2.756**	2.253**
Religious Attendance				
Less than once a week			—	—
Once or more a week			1.081*	1.104*
Religiosity over the life cycle				
Low in childhood and adulthood			—	—
Decreased since childhood			1.255+	1.457
Increased since childhood			1.813*	1.990*
High in childhood and adulthood			3.190**	3.077**
Background factors				
College-educated mother	-1.398*	-1.106+	-1.009+	-.914+
College-educated father	-.332	.408	.897+	1.255+
Married	.324	.366		
Children present in home	.930+	.619	-.149	-.171
Age in years	.032+	.041	.021	.030
Constant	15.692	17.149	11.720	12.459
R^2	.091	.175	.277	.306
Adjusted R^2	.075	.156	.251	.278

+p= < .10   *p= < .05   **p= < .01

traditional than native-born respondents, and their degree of gender traditionalism lessens with duration of U.S. residence. More recent immigrants, those who have lived here for less than 20 years, are considerably more gender traditional than native-born women, while immigrants who have lived in the United States for 20 years or more are somewhat more traditional.

Model 1 also considers the influences of marriage and parenting on women's gender ideologies, both of which typically encourage a more traditional division of labor in the home (e.g. Cassidy and Warren, 1996; Orbuch and Eyster, 1997).[39] Results indicate that marital status does not significantly affect women's ideologies, and presence of children has only a slight effect. In contrast, having a college-educated mother contributes significantly to respondents having more progressive gender beliefs. Socialization theory postulates that parents' educational attainment shapes offspring's gender orientations, and this is especially true for the impact of mother's education on daughter's beliefs (Kalmijn, 1994). Educated mothers are more egalitarian in their child rearing, expecting daughters as well as sons to be independent and leaders (Kelly, 1997).

Respondents' immigration and family characteristics alone do not sufficiently explain variations in their degree of gender traditionalism. Consequently, Models 2 and 3 consider the influences of education and culture on women's gender ideologies, respectively. Model 2 finds that college-educated respondents are considerably more

---

[39] Research suggests that presence of children in the home sufficiently measures the impact of parenting on women's gender ideologies. In the regression analysis, I tested the importance of children's age and found it was insignificant. Accordingly, I measure the impact of total number of children in the home, regardless of their ages.

egalitarian than women with less than a college degree, and the benefits associated with having a college-educated mother decrease slightly. One likely explanation for this latter finding is that educated mothers promote the educational attainments of their daughters, and it is the daughter's own education that leads her to reject traditional gender roles. Even when education is considered, duration of U.S. residence remains a robust predictor of gender traditionalism, which indicates the strength of indigenous cultural ties.

The impact of immigration status on women's gender ideologies suggests that particular cultural sources may mediate this relationship. Model 3 attempts to identify these sources by examining ethnic and religious links to gender traditionalism. Looking first at ethnicity, women involved in ethnic social circles are less egalitarian in their gender beliefs than are women without these relationships. Respondents with an Arab spouse and who share a majority of their social and organizational memberships with other Arabs have more traditional gender ideologies.

We can also speculate that these social and organizational memberships are religiously based, even though data do not distinguish women's particular organizational affiliations. Specifically, before religiosity measures are included in Model 3 (not shown), the influence of ethnic organizations on gender traditionalism is stronger and more statistically significant. The dimensions of religiosity that dampen this effect are belief in scriptural inerrancy and religiosity over the life cycle, a finding that confirms a strong association between religious involvement and traditional gender role attitudes (Heaton and Cornwall, 1989; Peek et al., 1991; Sherkat, 2000).

create a new variable for labor market region[40] because Arab Americans are not evenly distributed across the United States and because wages typically vary by residential location. Thus, labor market region represents both areas of greater opportunity provided by the labor market and ethnic enclaves.

Table 21 considers how these factors influence women's earnings. First, results in Model 1 show that duration of U.S. residence affects women's earnings. Newer arrivals, those who have lived in the United States for less than ten years, earn considerably less than do native-born women, while more settled immigrants (those who have resided in the United States for ten years or more) do not differ significantly from the native-born. There is insufficient information in Model 1 to explain this difference; variations in education may account for newer immigrant women's lesser earnings, or differences in women's labor market characteristics may be more important.

A more complicated pattern emerges when we look at regional differences in Model 1. Compared to women living in the South, respondents in the West and Northeast have significantly higher earnings, while women in the Midwest look similar to their southern counterparts. There are several possible explanations for these regional effects. One explanation is that wages and prices in the South are depressed, relative to other parts of the country, and

---

[40] Arab Americans are clustered in 20 metropolitan areas, with the six largest in Los Angeles, Chicago, Detroit, New York, and Washington DC (including Virginia and Maryland suburbs). I used this information to classify respondents into four regions: West, Midwest, Northeast, and South. Every region but the South represents areas of high Arab concentration.

another explanation is that there are fewer Arab co-ethnics in the South to pull women into the workforce (Cainkar, 1999). However, neither of these explanations account for why women in the Midwest look like women in the South (i.e., the Midwest offers greater economic opportunities and has higher concentrations of Arab Americans). The most likely explanation is that Arab Americans in the Midwest are of lower socio-economic status than Arab Americans in other parts of the country (Aswad, 1999). The three largest Arab-American communities in the Midwest are in Chicago, Detroit, and Dearborn, and several historical factors are associated with the class compositions of these ethnic communities.[41] Notably, the Arab Community Center for Economic and Social Services (ACCESS) is located in Dearborn, and immigrants in need of social services are drawn to this shelter. Arab immigrants are just as likely to settle in other Arab-American communities across the country, but those in need of social and economic support are more likely to settle in the Midwest (Aswad, 1999; Suleiman, 1999).[42]

One way to test the hypothesis that lower socio-economic status explains women's lower earnings in the Midwest is to include educational attainment in Model 2. Results show that college-educated respondents earn considerably more than women with less than a college degree, and U.S. credentials are more highly rewarded than foreign university qualifications.[43] Once we control for

---

[41] The auto industry boom in the 1970s drew many working class laborers to this region, and its consequent bust in the 1980s left many immigrants economically vulnerable.

[42] There are no regional differences in length of U.S. residence among women sampled.

[43] In alternate model specifications not shown, I created a new variable that identified three categories of educational attainment: no college

education, women's earnings in the Midwest become significantly higher than those in the South, which confirms the hypothesis that lower earnings seen in Model 1 reflect the lower educational attainment levels of many respondents in the Midwest. Moreover, when education is included in the analysis, the model fit improves substantially (26% of the variance in earnings is explained compared to 13% in Model 1). The continued importance of labor market region for earnings suggests that women are drawn into areas of greater economic opportunity. Finally, Model 2 finds that education does not account for disparities in immigrant women's earnings. Even when education and the source of education are considered, respondents with less than ten years of U.S. residence continue to earn substantially less than native-born women.

Since education cannot explain why newer immigrants earn less, Model 3 considers several labor market characteristics that may account for this difference. Specifically, earlier analysis found that foreign-born respondents are disproportionately located in lower occupational positions and have weaker labor force attachments than native-born women, and Model 3 considers whether these labor force characteristics explain the continued importance of immigration status for earnings. Looking first at the influence of labor force commitment on earnings, respondents who work full-time (40 to 49 hours a week) or more than full-time (50 or more hours a week) have higher earnings than women who work

---

credentials, foreign college credentials, and U.S. college credentials. Substantive findings were similar—compared to women with no credentials, all college-educated respondents earned higher incomes, and those with U.S. credentials fared slightly better than those with foreign education.

part-time (less than 40 hours a week). These results are not surprising, since yearly earnings are a mathematical function of wage rate multiplied by number of hours spent in the labor force (i.e., women who spend more time in the labor force are expected to have higher earnings).

The relationship between occupational attainment and women's earnings follows known patterns for U.S. men and women, generally (e.g. Kilbourne et al., 1994). Respondents in professional and managerial positions earn substantially more than do their counterparts in clerical and sales positions, self-employed respondents are similarly advantaged, while women in manufacturing and service occupations do not fare any better than women in clerical and sales positions. Results in Model 3 also indicate that labor force commitment and occupational attainment, in tandem, mediate the effects of education on earnings shown in Models 1 and 2. Educational attainment increases women's labor force commitments and provides the credentials needed to access higher-paying, prestigious occupations. Finally, differences in women's labor force commitments and occupational attainments explain why newer immigrants earn less than native-born women. We can deduce from earlier analyses that cultural factors restrict immigrant women's labor force commitments, which in turn, dampen their earnings.

Summary

Three findings are particularly striking in the analyses on Arab-American women's labor force activity. First, human capital increases women's labor force participation and earnings, which is consistent with research on U.S. men and women, in general. Education raises the costs of women remaining in the home, and this is especially true for respondents with a post-graduate or professional degree. Educated women, those with a bachelor's degree or higher, are more likely to participate in the paid labor force, work full-time, and earn higher incomes, compared to women with lower levels of education. Unlike the case for men, however, education does not clear entirely women's path to achievement. Arab-American women are subject to the universal conflict between women's domestic duties and their public sphere activities (Hochschild, 1989). Women's responsibilities as wives and mothers require they allocate more time to the home, and the presence of preschool children is especially demanding of women's resources. Moreover, these family influences are mediated by cultural factors—marital constraints operate through ethnic homogamy, and religiosity strengthens women's investments in the home. The multifaceted relationship between women's cultural affiliations, family constraints, and labor force participation brings us to the third important finding.

Beyond time constraints, the influence of family structure on labor force participation represents women's cultural obligations to the Arab family. Arab women are considered the foundation of the family, and their primary duties include childbearing and childrearing. These duties ultimately ensure the expansion and preservation of Arab ethnicity and weigh heavily on Arab-American women's labor force decisions. As the literal and symbolic bearers of culture, women may forego public sphere achievements to fulfill their duties to the family. Foreign-born women may feel even greater pressure to maintain their ethnicity and stave off Western cultural influences, many of which run counter to Arab norms and values (Haddad and Smith, 1996).

CHAPTER 6
Conclusion

This research on Arab-American women was motivated by two main objectives. The central objective of this study was to extend accepted models of female labor force participation to assess the significance of cultural factors in determining immigrant women's labor supply. With above-average levels of education, distinct cultural affiliations, and low rates of labor force participation, Arab-American women provide a unique opportunity to empirically compare conventional explanations for immigrant women's economic activity. The secondary objective was to challenge stereotypes of Arab-American women as restricted to the private sphere and add gender to existing research on Arab Americans. Several noteworthy findings emerge from this research, some of which are consistent with research on other U.S. women, and some of which provide additional insight into the importance of culture for immigrant women's economic incorporation.

Women's Achievements and the Universal Sisterhood

Many of the factors that influence Arab-American women's labor force participation also govern the labor supply of other groups of U.S. women. First, education has historically improved U.S. women's employment opportunities, and the same is true for Arab-American women. College-educated respondents reported higher labor force participation rates, greater earnings, lower fertility, and more egalitarian gender ideologies. The effects of education vary by nativity, with foreign-born respondents more likely to maximize their employment opportunities. This in part reflects the more recent emigration of highly educated women from the Middle East (Shakir, 1997). In sum, education is a valuable asset for women because it improves prospects for their achievements at the individual, household, and societal levels.

While education improved Arab-American women's social positions dramatically, it did not remove all barriers to gender equality. Similar to women globally, Arab-American women remained responsible for their labor in the domestic sphere. Married respondents and those with children in the home maintained a more traditional gender division of labor, and education did not alter these dynamics. These findings are not unique to Arab-American women; women's reproductive abilities and the subsequent social prescription of female domesticity have historically limited their public sphere activities. Traditional gender role attitudes, promoted through such cultural institutions as religion and ethnicity, sustain these gender differences.

Beyond these similarities with U.S. women, Arab-American women's achievements are distinguished by their unique cultural circumstances. The family is central in Arab culture, and the cultural basis for women's family obligations was evidenced throughout the analyses. For example, marital constraints on women's labor force participation operated through Arab spouses, and the restrictive impact of preschool children was mediated by women's degree of religiosity.

The Gendered Consequences of Culture

One of the more important findings of this research concerns the impact of cultural factors on Arab-American women's labor force participation. Foreign-born women, particularly those who have lived in the United States for less than 15 years, are less likely than the native-born to participate in the paid labor force, and this difference is explained by ethnic and religious differences between the groups. Arab immigrant women come to America with cultural traits that distinguish them from native-born women; they are more likely to have an Arab husband, to believe in scriptural inerrancy, and to support patriarchal gender roles. Once these cultural factors are considered, the impact of nativity on Arab-American women's labor force participation disappears. These measures also appear to explain why foreign-born women with 15 years or more of U.S. residency have lower rates of full-time employment, compared to native-born respondents. They do not, however, account for the lower rates of labor force commitment among more recent immigrant arrivals. This unexplained variation may reflect the effects of discrimination on the employment opportunities of Arab immigrant women (Moore, 1995).

Notably, not all dimensions of Arab culture constrain female labor force participation. For example, this study finds little support for stereotypes of women's subjugation in Islam. Nearly one-half of women sampled are Muslim, but Islam alone does not appear to dissuade women's public sphere participation—in the final analysis, Muslim affiliation has little or no effect on respondents' labor force participation and commitment. Gender traditionalism has a much greater effect, but contrary to popular stereotypes, being a Muslim is not synonymous with an Arab woman's belief in traditional gender roles (Haddad and Smith, 1996; Read, 2003).

Perhaps most striking is the significance of homogamy for women's employment. The restrictive effect of an Arab spouse remains robust even after gender traditionalism is considered—a finding that indicates a structural dimension of culture not captured by more subjective measures. Though some may interpret the effect of homogamy as bolstering stereotypes of Arab men as oppressive and Arab women as confined to the domestic sphere, ethnographic studies of U.S. Muslim and Arab-American families consistently find that women base their employment decisions on a myriad of economic and social factors. Like women, generally, they balance gender role expectations with the demands of daily life (Bartkowski and Read, 2003; Read and Bartkowski, 2000). Endogamous marriages are often accompanied by extended kinship networks that can add to these demands, requiring greater commitment to labor-intensive ethnic practices, such as frequent family gatherings and obligations to prepare traditional meals for family members (Aswad and Bilge, 1996). Studies also find that the presence of in-laws can serve to enforce traditional gender role expectations (e.g., Read and Bartkowski, 2000). Future work could explore this possibility.

A different interpretation is that homogamy symbolizes alternative family patterns among Arab immigrants (c.f., Foner, 1997). Rather than viewing family arrangements in the traditional, western sense (i.e., gendered division of labor), individual family obligations may represent broader cultural norms on family stability (Joseph, 1999). Arab-American women may be reacting to forces that situate the Arab-American family in opposition to western influences. Like other immigrant groups, Arab Americans are concerned with the breakdown in the American family and are committed to preserving their ethnicity, which centers largely on family stability (Haddad and Smith, 1996). Accordingly, women's individual duties to the family may carry symbolic consequences for the Arab family collectively, and foreign-born women, with greater ties to indigenous values, may feel more accountable than native-born women for sustaining Arab ethnicity in the United States.

Summary and Future Research

Though not without limitations, this study points to important cultural factors not captured in economic models of female labor force participation. At least for Arab-American women, religiosity, gender traditionalism, and homogamy have important consequences for their labor force decisions. The significance of an Arab spouse is especially noteworthy and suggests promising avenues of future research. Most large data sets contain information on homogamy, and future studies should examine whether in-marriage is similarly restrictive for other groups of immigrant women. Research should also attempt to understand the mechanisms by which homogamy influences women's entry into the labor force. The presence of a co-ethnic spouse is isolated as a determinant of Arab-American women's labor force participation; however, the data do not allow for an examination of family decision-making processes.

Finally, future work should expand some of the current findings to a more representative sample of Arab-American women. Though census data contain insufficient information on the cultural variables of interest for this research, it remains the most reliable source for making intra- and inter-group comparisons. Decennial data are particularly useful because they contain larger numbers of smaller immigrant groups, such as Arab Americans. As a population of increasing size and importance, future research should attempt to distinguish the experiences of Arab Americans from those of other immigrant populations and from the majority white population.

Appendix A

An important goal of this study is to identify differences among Arab-American women. So, I'd like to begin by asking you some questions about Arab ethnicity. (Please circle ONE response for each question):

1. Of your five closest friends, how many are of Arab ethnicity?
   1 None of them
   2 One or two of them
   3 Three or four of them
   4 All of them

2. Now thinking of various social groups and organizations that you belong to, how many members share your ethnic background?
   1 None of them
   2 Some of them
   3 Most of them
   4 All of them
   9 Unsure/not applicable

3. In a typical week, how often are Arabic meals prepared in your home?
   1 Never
   2 Rarely
   3 Sometimes
   4 Frequently

4. How well do you speak Arabic?
    1   Not at all
    2   Know a few words and phrases
    3   Speak it conversationally
    4   Speak it fluently

5. How closely do you follow Middle Eastern news?
    1   Not closely at all
    2   Not very closely
    3   Somewhat closely
    4   Very closely

6. If someone asked you about your ethnicity, how would you describe yourself?
    1   Arab
    2   American
    3   Arab American
    4   Other (specify): _____

Now I'd like to ask you some questions about your family and work experiences.

7. How many of the 52 weeks in 1999 did you work at a paid job either part-time or full- time? Include paid vacations and paid sick leave as time spent working.
    1   0 Weeks / Did not work
    2   1-19 Weeks
    3   20-29 Weeks
    4   30-39 Weeks
    5   40-52 Weeks

8. Now thinking of a typical week in 1999, how many hours did you work at a paid job?
    1   0 Hours / Did not work
    2   1-19 Hours
    3   20-39 Hours
    4   40-49 Hours
    5   50 Hours or more

9. **How important to you is achievement in your job?**
    1   Very important
    2   Moderately important
    3   Not very important
    4   Not at all important
    9   Not applicable / Not working

10. **Which of the following best describes your current occupation?** **(Circle ALL that apply)**
    1   Part-time homemaker
    2   Full-time homemaker
    3   Manufacturing / Service
    4   Clerical / Sales
    5   Professional / Managerial
    6   Student
    7   Retired
    8   Other (specify): _____

11. **Beside yourself, who currently resides in your home?** **(Circle ALL that apply)**
    1   Husband
    2   His parent(s)
    3   Your parent(s)
    4   Children
    5   Other (specify): _____
    6   No one else

12. **How many children in the following age categories currently live in your home?**

    <u>NUMBER OF CHILDREN</u>   (If none, write "0")
    _____ under 5 years of age
    _____ 5 to 13
    _____ 14 to 17
    _____ 18 and over

13. **In general, how satisfied are you with your marriage?**
     1   Very satisfied
     2   Moderately satisfied
     3   Not very satisfied
     4   Not at all satisfied
     9   Not applicable / Not married

14. **Please indicate your work status during each of the following time periods. If a situation does not apply to you, please circle "Doesn't Apply." (Circle ONE number for each time period):**

	Not Employed	Employed Part-time	Employed Full-time	Doesn't Apply
After marriage and before children:	1	2	3	9
Children under school age at home:	1	2	3	9
After youngest child started school:	1	2	3	9
After children left home:	1	2	3	9

15. **People make various decisions on a daily basis. Sometimes these decisions are made *alone*, sometimes they are made *jointly with others*, and sometimes they are made *by other people*. Below is a list of common life decisions. On a scale of 1 to 7, where 1 means *alone* and 7 means *by others*, please circle the number that best describes how you made your *final* decision. If a situation does not apply to you, please circle "Doesn't Apply." (Circle ONE number for each time period):**

Whether you held a job: 1--------2--------3--------4--------5--------6--------7   9
                     Alone   Jointly   By others   Doesn't Apply

Whether you got a college education:
                    1--------2--------3--------4--------5--------6--------7   9
                    Alone   Jointly   By others   Doesn't Apply

The number of children to have:

```
1--------2--------3--------4--------5--------6--------7          9
    Alone            Jointly      By others    Doesn't Apply
```

Where your children attend school:

```
1--------2--------3--------4--------5--------6--------7          9
    Alone            Jointly      By others    Doesn't Apply
```

Where the household income is spent:

```
1--------2--------3--------4--------5--------6--------7          9
    Alone            Jointly      By others    Doesn't Apply
```

Please feel free to elaborate on any of these decisions:

_____

_____

_____

Another important purpose of this study is to learn more about religious diversity among Arab Americans.

16. What is your current religious affiliation? (Specify sect if appropriate)

    1   Muslim _____

    2   Christian _____

    3   Jewish

    4   Other (specify) _____

    5   None

    6

17. In what religion, if any, were you raised? (Specify sect if appropriate)

    1   Muslim _____

    2   Christian _____

    3   Jewish

    4   Other (specify) _____

    5   None

18. In general, how religious would you say you are?
1   Not at all religious
2   Not very religious
3   Somewhat religious
4   Very religious

19. During your teenage years, how religious was your family?
1   Not at all religious
2   Not very religious
3   Moderately religious
4   Very religious

20. Now thinking of last year, how often do you read religious materials?
1   Never
2   A few times
3   About once a month
4   Two or three times a month
7   About once a week
8   More than once a week
9   Nearly everyday

21. How often did you attend religious services?
1   Never
2   A few times
3   About once a month
4   Two or three times a month
5   About once a week
6   More than once a week
7   Nearly everyday

22. Do you agree or disagree with the following statement:
"The holy book of my religion is the literal word of God."
1   Strongly agree
2   Agree
3   Neither agree nor disagree
4   Disagree
5   Strongly disagree

Relatively little is known about Arab-American women's political opinions. So, now I'd like to ask you about your attitudes toward various political issues.

23. **How important is a Presidential candidate's position on the Middle East in gaining your support?**
1 Very important
2 Moderately important
3 Not very important
4 Not at all important

24. **How important is a Presidential candidate's position on women's issues in gaining your support?**
1 Very important
2 Moderately important
3 Not very important
4 Not at all important

25. **How likely would you be to vote for a female Presidential candidate, all else being equal?**
1 Very likely
2 Somewhat likely
3 Not very likely
4 Not at all likely

26. **For each of the groups below, indicate whether you think they have too much power, too little power, or just the right amount of influence in American life and politics. (Circle ONE number for each group):**

	Too Much Influence	Too Little Influence	Just the Right Amount
Men as a group:	1	2	3
Women as a group:	1	2	3
Christian groups:	1	2	3
Jewish groups:	1	2	3
Arab-American groups:	1	2	3

27. In addition to political attitudes, I would like to ask your opinions on other various topics. Please indicate whether you agree or disagree with each of the following statements. (Circle ONE number for each statement):

	Strongly Agree	Agree	Unsure	Disagree	Strongly Disagree
Women should be allowed to lead Religious services.	1	2	3	4	5
Preschool children will likely suffer if their mother is employed.	1	2	3	4	5
Parents should encourage just as much independence in their daughters as in their sons.	1	2	3	4	5
It is better for everyone if the husband makes the major decisions for the family.	1	2	3	4	5
If a husband and wife both work full-time they should share in household tasks equally.	1	2	3	4	5
If you work hard enough, you can achieve anything in the U.S.	1	2	3	4	5
The U.S. still needs a strong woman's movement to bring about equality.	1	2	3	4	5

Finally, I'd like to ask you some questions about yourself to help interpret the results.

28. In which countries were the following people born? (Specify in the spaces provided)

    Yourself: _____
    Mother: _____
    Father: _____
    Mother's parents: _____
    Father's parents: _____

29. **What is the highest level of education you have completed?**
1 Less than high school
2 High school graduate
3 Some college
4 College graduate
5 Post graduate / professional degree

30. **Where did you obtain your college education?**
1 Completely abroad
2 Mainly abroad
3 Mainly in the United States
4 Completely in the United States
9 Not applicable

31. **What is the highest level of education your *father* completed?**
1 Less than high school
2 High school graduate
3 Some college
4 College graduate
5 Post graduate / professional degree

32. **What is the highest level of education your *mother* completed?**
1 Less than high school
2 High school graduate
3 Some college
4 College graduate
5 Post graduate / professional degree

33. **What is your political party preference here in the U.S.?**
1 Democrat
2 Republican
3 Independent
4 Other (specify): _____
5 None

34. What was your approximate INDIVIDUAL income from paid employment during 1999?
1   Less than $15,000
2   $15,000 TO $24,999
3   $25,000 TO $34,999
4   $35,000 TO $44,999
5   $45,000 TO $54,999
6   $55,000 TO $64,999
7   $65,000 TO $74,999
8   $75,000 OR HIGHER
9   Not applicable / Did not work

35. What was your approximate FAMILY income from paid employment during 1999?
1   Less than $20,000
2   $20,000 to $39,999
3   $40,000 to $59,999
4   $60,000 to $79,999
5   $80,000 to $99,999
6   $100,000 or higher

36. In what year were you born? _____

37. In what year did you first come to the United States? _____

38. What is your current marital status?
1   Never married
2   Married
3   Divorced
4   Separated
5   Widowed

39. What is the highest level of education your spouse completed?
1   Less than high school
2   High school graduate
3   Some college
4   College graduate
5   Post graduate / professional degree
8   Not applicable

40. Please specify your spouse's ethnic heritage.

Current spouse:
1. Arab
2. American
3. Jewish
4. Other (specify): _____
9. Not applicable

Former spouse:
1. Arab
2. American
3. Jewish
4. Other
9. Not applicable

41. Please specify your spouse's religion. (Specify sect if appropriate)

Current spouse:
1. Muslim _____
2. Christian _____
3. Jewish
4. Other (specify): _____
5. None
9. Not applicable

Former spouse:
1. Muslim _____
2. Christian _____
3. Jewish
4. Other (specify): _____
5. None
9. Not applicable

Please feel free to comment or elaborate on any of the questions in the space below. If you are interested in being contacted for possible follow-up interviews in the future, please provide contact information here (phone or e-mail):

Thank you for your participation. Please return the survey in the pre-paid envelope.

Appendix B

VARIABLES	MEASURES
Dependent Variables	
Labor force participation	1=Employed, 0=other
Labor force commitment	1=Employed full-time, 0=other
Independent Variables	
<u>Cultural Factors</u>	
Nativity	
(Native-born)	Reference category
FB, U.S. resident < 15 years	1=Less than 15 years, 0=other
FB, U.S. resident > 15 years	1=15 years or more, 0=other
Religious affiliation	1=Muslim, 0=other
Belief in scriptural inerrancy	1=Strongly believe or believe, 0=other
Religiosity over life cycle	1=High in childhood and adulthood, 0=other
Homogamy	
(Not married)	Reference category
Arab spouse	1=Married to an Arab, 0=other
Non-Arab spouse	1=Married to non-Arab, 0=other
Gender traditionalism	10-item index, Cronbach's alpha=.734

VARIABLES	MEASURES
Educational attainment	
(Less than Bachelor's degree)	Reference category
Bachelor's degree	1=Bachelor's degree, 0=other
Post-graduate or professional degree	1=Post-graduate degree, 0=other
Background Factors	
Additional family income	
Low resources	1=< $20,000 a year, 0=other
(Medium resources)	1=$20,000 to $50,000 a year, 0=other
High resources	1=> $50,000 a year, 0=other
Labor market region	
(South)	Reference category
East	1=yes, 0=other
West	1=yes, 0=other
Midwest	1=yes, 0=other
Children in home:	
(No children)	Reference category
Less than 5 years old	1=Less than 5 years old, 0=other
5 years and older	1=5 years and older, 0=other
Adults in home	1=yes, 0=no
Age in years	Continuous and quadratic terms

( ) Denotes reference category for polytomous variables

References

Abdul-Rauf, Muhammad. 1977. *The Islamic View of Women and the Family.* New York: Exposition Press.

Ajrouch, Kristine. 1999. "Family and Ethnic Identity in an Arab-American Community." Pp. 129-39 in *Arabs in America: Building a New Future,* edited by Michael W. Suleiman. Philadelphia: Temple University Press.

Alon, Sigal, Debra Donahoe, and Marta Tienda. 2001. "The Effects of Early Work Experience on Young Women's Labor Force Attachment." Social Forces 79, 3:1005-34.

Aswad, Barbara C. 1999. "Attitudes of Arab Immigrants Toward Welfare." Pp. 177-91 in *Arabs in America: Building a New Future,* edited by Michael W. Suleiman. Philadelphia: Temple University Press.

_____. 1994. "Attitudes of Immigrant Women and Men in the Dearborn Area Toward Women's Employment and Welfare." Pp. 501-19 in Yvonne Yazbeck Haddad and Jane Idleman Smith, eds., *Muslim Communities in North America.* Albany: State University of New York Press.

Aswad, Barbara C. and Barbara Bilge (eds). 1996. *Family and Gender among American Muslims: Issues Facing Middle Eastern Immigrants and their Descendants.* Philadelphia: Temple University Press.

Axinn, William G. 1993. "The Effects of Children's Schooling on Fertility Limitation." Population Studies 47, 3:481-93.

Baca Zinn, Maxine, and Bonnie Thornton Dill. 1996. "Theorizing Difference from Multiracial Feminism." *Feminist Studies* 22:321-31.

Bartkowski, John P. and Jen'nan Ghazal Read. 2003. "Veiled Submission: Gender, Power, and Identity among Evangelical and Muslim Women in the U.S." *Qualitative Sociology* 26, 1:71-92.

Bernhardt, Annette, Martina Morris, and Mark S. Handcock. 1995. "Women's Gains or Men's Losses? A Closer Look at the Shrinking Gender Gap in Earnings." *American Journal of Sociology* 101, 2:302-28.

Bilge, Barbara and Barbara C. Aswad. 1996. "Introduction." Pp. 1-16 in *Family and Gender among American Muslims: Issues Facing Middle Eastern Immigrants and their Descendants,* edited by Barbara C. Aswad and Barbara Bilge. Philadelphia: Temple University Press.

Blumberg, Rae Lesser. 1984. "A General Theory of Gender Stratification." Pp. 23-97 in *Sociological Theory*, Jossey-Bass Social and Behavioral Science Series, edited by Randall Collins. San Francisco: Jossey-Bass Publishers.

Bozorgmehr, Mehdi. 1998. "From Iranian Studies to Studies of Iranians in the United States." *Iranian Studies* 31, 1:5-30.

Bozorgmehr, Mehdi, Claudia Der-Martirosian, and Georges Sabagh. 1996. "Middle Easterners: A New Kind of Immigrant." Pp. 345-75 in *Ethnic Los Angeles*, edited by Roger Waldinger and Mehdi Bozorgmehr. New York: Russell Sage Foundation.

Browne, Irene. 1997. "Explaining the Black-White Gap in Labor Force Participation among Women Heading Households." *American Sociological Review* 62:236-52.

Cainkar, Louise. 1999. "The Deteriorating Ethnic Safety Net Among Arab Immigrants in Chicago." Pp. 192-208 in *Arabs in America: Building a New Future*, edited by Michael W. Suleiman. Philadelphia: Temple University Press.

_____. 1996. "Immigrant Palestinian Women Evaluate Their Lives." Pp. 41-59 in Barbara C. Aswad and Barbara Bilge, eds., *Family and Gender among American Muslims: Issues Facing Middle Eastern Immigrants and Their Descendants*. Philadelphia: Temple University Press.

Cassidy, Margaret L. and Bruce O. Warren. 1996. "Family Employment Status and Gender Role Attitudes: A Comparison of Women and Men College Graduates." *Gender & Society* 10, 3:312-29.

Chafetz, Janet Saltzman. 1988. *Feminist Sociology: An Overview of Contemporary Theories*. Itasca, Illinois: F.E. Peacock Publishers, Inc.

Collins, Patricia Hill. 1991. *Black Feminist Thought: Knowledge, Consciousness, and the Politics of Empowerment*. New York: Routledge.

Cooney, Rosemary S. and Vilma Ortiz. 1983. "Nativity, National Origin, and Hispanic Female Participation in the Labor Force." *Social Science Quarterly* 64, 3:510-23.

Cotter, David A., JoAnn DeFiore, Joan M. Hermsen, Brenda Marsterller Kowalewski, and Reeve Vanneman. 1998. "The Demand for Female Labor." *American Journal of Sociology* 103, 6:1673-99.

Curtis, James E., Edward G. Grabb, and Douglas E. Baer. 1992. "Voluntary Association Membership in Fifteen Countries: A Comparative Analysis." *American Sociological Review* 57:139-52.

Dallafar, A. 1996. "The Iranian Ethnic Economy in Los Angeles: Gender and Entrepreneurship." Pp 107-128 in *Family and Gender among American Muslims: Issues Facing Middle Eastern Immigrants and their Descendants*, edited by B.C. Aswad and B. Bilge. Philadelphia: Temple University Press.

_____. 1994. "Iranian Women as Immigrant Entrepreneurs." *Gender & Society,* 8:541-561.

Darity, William Jr., David K. Guilkey, and William Winfrey. 1996. "Explaining Differences in Economic Performance Among Racial and Ethnic Groups in the USA: The Data Examined." *American Journal of Economics and Sociology* 55, 4:411-25.

Dill, Bonnie Thornton. 1979. "The Dialectics of Black Womanhood." *Signs* 4, 3:543-55.

Dodoo, F. Nii-Amoo. 1997. "Assimilation Differences among Africans in America." *Social Forces* 76, 2:527-46.

Ebaugh, Helen Rose and Janet Saltzman Chafetz. 2000. *Religion and the New Immigrants: Continuities and Adaptations in Immigrant Congregations.* New York: Altamira Press.

_____. 1999. "Agents for Cultural Reproduction and Structural Change: The Ironic Role of Women in Immigrant Religious Institutions." *Social Forces* 78, 2:585-612.

Edmonston, Barry and Jeffrey S. Passel. 1994. "Ethnic Demography: U.S. Immigration and Ethnic Variations." Pp. 1-30 in *Immigration and Ethnicity: The Integration of America's Newest Arrivals.* Washington, DC: The Urban Institute Press.

El-Badry, S. 1994. "The Arab-American Market." *American Demographics* 16, 1:22-31.

Esposito, John L. 1998. "Women in Islam and Muslim Societies." Introduction to Yvonne Yazbeck Haddad and John L. Esposito, eds., *Islam, Gender, and Social Change.* New York: Oxford University Press.

Feagin, Joe R. and Karyn D. McKinney. 2003. *The Many Costs of Racism.* Lanham, Maryland: Rowman & Littlefield Publishers, Inc.

Featherman, David L. and Robert M. Hauser. 1976. "Sexual Inequalities and Socio-economic Achievement in the U.S., 1962-1973." *American Sociological Review* 41, 3:462-83.

Fejgin, Naomi. 1995. "Factors Contributing to the Academic Excellence of American Jewish and Asian Students." *Sociology of Education* 68:18-30.

Foner, Nancy, Rubén G. Rumbaut, and Steven J. Gold (eds). 2000. *Immigration Research For a New Century: Multidisciplinary Perspectives.* New York: Russell Sage Foundation.

Fong, Lina Y.S. 1997. "Asian-American Women: An Understudied Minority." *Journal of Sociology and Social Welfare* 24, 1: 91-111.

Frazier, E. Franklin. 1966. *The Negro Family in the United States.* Chicago: University of Chicago Press.

GhanneaBassiri, K. 1997.   *Competing Visions of Islam in the United States: A Study of Los Angeles.* Westport, Connecticut: Greenwood Press.

Glass, Jennifer. 1992. "Housewives and Employed Wives: Demographic and Attitudinal Change, 1972-1986." *Journal of Marriage and the Family* 54, 3:559-569.

Glazer, Nathan and Daniel Moynihan. 1963. *Beyond the Melting Pot.* Harvard University Press.

Glenn, Evelyn Nakano. 1992. "From servitude to service work: Historical continuities in the racial division of paid reproductive labor." *Signs* 18, 1:1-43.

Greenless, C.S. and R. Saenz. 1999. "Determinants of Employment of Recently Arrived Mexican Immigrant Wives." *International Migration Review* 33, 2:354-377.

Haddad, Yvonne Yazbeck. 1998. "Islam and Gender: Dilemmas in the Changing Arab World." Pp. 3-29 in *Islam, Gender, and Social,* edited by Yvonne Yazbeck Haddad and John L. Esposito. New York: Oxford University Press.

_____. 1991. *The Muslims of America,* edited by Yvonne Yazbeck Haddad. New York: Oxford University Press.

Haddad, Yvonne Y. and Adair T. Lummis. 1987. *Islamic Values in the United States: A Comparative Study.* New York: Oxford University Press.

Haddad, Yvonne Y. and Jane I. Smith. 1996. "Islamic Values among American Muslims." Pp. 19-40 in Barbara C. Aswad and Barbara Bilge, eds., *Family and Gender among American Muslims: Issues Facing Middle Eastern Immigrants and Their Descendants.* Philadelphia: Temple University Press.

Hartman, Harriet and Moshe Hartman. 1996a. *Gender Equality and American Jews.* Albany: State University New York Press.

_____. 1996b. "More Jewish, Less Jewish: Implications for Education and Labor Force Characteristics." *Sociology of Religion* 57, 2:175-93.

Hawkins, B. Denise. 1993. "Socio-economic Family Background Still a Significant Influence on SAT Scores." *Black Issues in Higher Education*, September: 14-16.

Hayani, Ibrahim. 1999. "Arabs in Canada: Assimilation or Integration?" Pp. 284-303 in *Arabs in America: Building a New Future*, edited by Michael W. Suleiman. Philadelphia: Temple University Press.

Heaton, Tim and Marie C. Cornwall. 1989. "Religious Group Variation in the Socioeconomic Status and Family Behavior of Women." *Journal for the Scientific Study of Religion* 28, 3:283-299.

Hertel, Bradley R. and Michael Hughes. 1987. "Religious Affiliation, Attendance, and Support for 'Pro-Family' Issues in the United States." *Social Forces* 65:858-82.

Hijab, Nadia. 1988. *Womanpower: The Arab Debate on Women at Work.* New York: Cambridge University Press.

Huber, Joan and Glenna Spitze. 1981. "Wives' Employment, Household Behaviors, and Sex-Role Attitudes." *Social Forces* 60, 1:150-69.

Joseph, Suad. 1999. "Introduction." *Intimate Selving in Arab Families: Gender, Self, and Identity,* edited by S. Joseph. New York: Syracuse University Press.

Kahn, Joan R. and Leslie A. Whittington. 1996. "The Labor Supply of Latinas in the USA: Comparing Labor Force Participation, Wages, and Hours Worked with Anglo and Black Women." *Population Research and Policy Review* 15:45-73.

Kalmijn, K. 1996. "The socioeconomic assimilation of Caribbean American blacks." *Social Forces* 74:911-930.

Keck, Lois T. 1989. "Egyptian Americans in the Washington, DC Area." Pp. 103-26 in *Arab Americans: Continuity and Change*, edited by Baha Abu-Laban and Michael W. Suleiman. Belmont, Massachusetts: Association of Arab-American University Graduates, Inc.

Kerber, Linda K. 1988. "Separate Spheres, Female Worlds, Woman's Place: A Rhetoric of Women's History." *Journal of American History* 75, 1: 9-39.

Kilbourne, Barbara, Paula England, and Kurt Beron. 1994. "Effects of Individual, Occupational, and Industrial Characteristics on Earnings: Intersections of Race and Gender." *Social Forces* 72, 4:1149-76.

Lee, Sharon M. 1994. "Poverty and the U.S. Asian Population." *Social Science Quarterly* 75, 3:541-59.

Lehrer, Evelyn L. 1995. "The Effects of Religion on the Labor Supply of Married Women." *Social Science Research* 24, 3:281-301.

Lehrer, Evelyn L. and C. Chiswick. 1993. "Religion as a Determinant of Marital Stability." *Demography* 30, 3:385-404.

Lewis, Oscar. 1961. *The Children of Sachez*. New York: Random House.

Liebow, Elliot. 1967. *Tally's Corner*. Boston: Little Brown.

Manza, Jeff and Clem Brooks. 1998. "The Gender Gap in U.S. Presidential Elections: When? Why? Implications?" *American Journal of Sociology* 103, 5:1235-66.

Marini, Margaret Mooney. 1989. "Sex Differences in Earnings in the United States." *Annual Review of Sociology* 15:343-80.

Massey, Douglas S. and Nancy A. Denton. 1993. *American Apartheid*. Cambridge: Harvard University Press.

Moore, Kathleen M. 1999. "A Closer Look at Anti-Terrorism Law: *American-Arab Anti-Discrimination Committee V. Reno* and the Construction of Aliens' Rights." Pp. 84-99 in *Arabs in America: Building a New Future*, edited by Michael W. Suleiman. Philadelphia: Temple University Press.

Moore, Kathleen.M. 1995. *Al-Mughtarib-un: American Law and the Transformation of Muslim Life in the United States*. Albany: State University of New York Press.

Naff, Alixa. 1994. "The Early Arab Immigrant Experience." Pp. 23-35 in *The Development of Arab-American Identity*, edited by Ernest McCarus. Ann Arbor: The University of Michigan Press.

Oliver, Melvin L. and Thomas Shapiro. 1995. *Black Wealth, White Wealth: A New Perspective on Racial Inequality*. New York: Routledge.

Orbuch, Terri L. and Sandra L. Eyster. 1997. "Division of Household Labor among Black Couples and White Couples." *Social Forces* 76, 1:301-32.

Ortiz, Vilma and Rosemary Santana Cooney. 1984. "Sex-Role Attitudes and Labor Force Participation among Young Hispanic Females and Non-Hispanic White Females." *Social Science Quarterly* 65, 2:392-400.

Peek, Charles W., George D. Lowe, and L. Susan Williams. 1991. "Gender and God's Word: Another Look at Religious Fundamentalism and Sexism." *Social Forces* 69, 4:1205-22.

Plutzer, Eric. 1988. "Work life, Family life, and Women's Support of Feminism." *American Sociological Review* 53, 4: 640-49.

Portes, Alejandro and Ruben Rumbaut. 2001. Legacies: The Story of the Immigrant Second Generation. Berkeley: University of California Press.

_____. 1996. *Immigrant America: A Portrait, 2nd edition.* Berkeley: University of California Press.

Pulcini, Theodore. 1993. "Trends in Research on Arab Americans." *Journal of American Ethnic History* 12, 4:27-60.

Read, Jen'nan Ghazal. 2004. "Cultural Influences on Ethnic Women's Labor Force Participation: The Case of Arab Americans." *International Migration Review* 38 (forthcoming).

_____. 2003. "The Sources of Gender Role Attitudes among Christian and Muslim Arab-American Women." *Sociology of Religion* 64, 2:207-222.

_____. 2002. "Challenging Myths of Muslim Women: The Influence of Islam on Arab-American Women's Labor Force Activity." *Muslim World* 96:19-38.

Read, Jen'nan Ghazal and John P. Bartkowski. 2000. "To Veil or Not to Veil? A Case Study of Identity Negotiation among Muslim Women in Austin, Texas." *Gender & Society* 14, 3:395-417.

Rumbaut, Ruben and Alejandro Portes (eds). 2001. *Ethnicities: Children of Immigrants in America.* Berkeley: University of California Press.

Sabagh, George and Mehdi Bozorgmehr. 1994. "Secular Immigrants: Religiosity and Ethnicity among Iranian Muslims in Los Angeles." Pp. 445-73 *in Muslim Communities in North America,* edited by Yvonne Yazbeck Haddad and Jane Idleman Smith. Albany: State University of New York Press.

Sanday, Peggy. 1974. "Female Status in the Public Domain." Pp. 189-206 in *Woman, Culture, and Society,* edited by Michelle Zimbalist Rosaldo and Louise Lamphere. Stanford: Stanford University Press.

Schoeni, R.F. 1998. "Labor Market Outcomes of Immigrant Women in the United States: 1970 to 1990." *International Migration Review* 32, 1:57-77.

Shaheen, Jack G. 1994. "Arab Images in American Comic Books." *Journal of Popular Culture* 28:123-33.

Shakir, Evelyn. 1997. *Bint Arab: Arab and Arab American Women in the United States.* Westport, Connecticut: Praeger.

Sherkat, Darren E. 2000. "'That They Be Keepers of the Home': The Effect of Conservative Religion on Early and Late Transitions into Housewifery." *Review of Religious Research* 41, 3:344-58.

Sokoloff, Natalie. 1992. *Black Women and White Women in the Professions.* New York: Routledge.

Sorensen, Glorian and Lois M. Verbrugge. 1987. "Women, Work, and Health." Annual Review of Public Health 8:235-51.

Sowell, Thomas. 1981. Ethnic America. New York: Basic Books.

Stier, Haya. 1991. "Immigrant Women Go to Work: Analysis of Immigrant Wives' Labor Supply for Six Asian Groups." *Social Science Quarterly* 72, 1:67-82.

Stier, Haya and Marta Tienda. 1992. "Family, Work, and Women: The Labor Supply of Hispanic Immigrant Wives." *International Migration Review* 26:1291-1313.

Suleiman, Michael W. 1999. "Introduction: The Arab Immigrant Experience." Pp. 1-21 in *Arabs in America: Building a New Future*, edited by Michael W. Suleiman. Philadelphia: Temple University Press.

Suleiman, Michael W. and Baha Abu-Laban. 1989.
"Introduction." Pp. 1-13 in *Arab Americans: Continuity and Change*, edited by Baha Abu-Laban and Michael W. Suleiman. Belmont, Massachusetts: Association of Arab-American University Graduates, Inc.

Swanson, Jon C. 1996. "Ethnicity, Marriage, and Role Conflict: The Dilemma of a Second-Generation Arab-American." Pp. 241-49 in *Family and Gender among American Muslims: Issues Facing Middle Eastern Immigrants and their Descendants,* edited by Barbara C. Aswad and Barbara Bilge. Philadelphia: Temple University Press.

Terry, Janice J. 1985. "Mistaken Identity: Arab Stereotypes in Popular Writing." Washington, DC: American-Arab Affairs Council.

Thornton, Arland, Duane F. Alwin, and Donald Camburn. 1983. "Causes and Consequences of Sex-Role Attitudes and Attitude Changes." *American Sociological Review* 48, 2:211-21.

Toubia, Nahid, ed. 1988. *Women of the Arab World: The Coming Challenge.* London: Zed Books Ltd.

U.S. Bureau of the Census. 1998a. *Statistical Abstract of the U.S. 1998.* 118th edition. Washington, DC: U.S. Government Printing Office.

_____. 1998b. *Current Population Reports, Money Income in the US: 1997.* Washington, DC: U.S. Government Printing Office.

_____. 1990a. *Census of Population and Housing. Public-Use Microdata Samples.* Washington, DC: U.S. Government Printing Office.

_____. 1990b. *Census of Population and Housing, CP-3-2, Ancestry of the Population of the United States, 1990.* Washington, DC: U.S. Government Printing Office.

_____. 1990c. *Census of Population and Housing, CP-2-1, Social and Economic Characteristics, 1990.* Washington, DC: U.S. Government Printing Office.

Walbridge, Linda S. 1997. *Without Forgetting the Imam: Lebanese Shi'ism in an American Community.* Detroit: Wayne State University Press.

Waters, Mary. 1999. *Black Identities.* Cambridge: Harvard University Press.

_____. 1990. *Ethnic Options: Choosing Identities in America.* Berkeley: University of California Press.

Wilcox, Clyde and Ted G. Jelen. 1991. "The Effects of Employment and Religion on Women's Feminist Attitudes." *The International Journal for the Psychology of Religion* 1, 3:161-71.

Wilder, Esther I. and William H. Walters. 1998. "Ethnic and Religious Components of the Jewish Income Advantage, 1969-1989." *Sociological Inquiry* 68, 3:426-36.

Xu, Wu and Ann Leffler. 1992. "Gender and Race Effects on Occupational Prestige, Segregation, and Earnings." *Gender & Society* 6, 3:376-92.

Yamanaka, Keiko and Kent McClelland. 1994. "Earning the model-minority image: Diverse strategies of economic adaptation by Asian-American women." *Ethnic and Racial Studies* 17, 1:79-114.

Zogby, John. 2001. A Poll of Arab Americans since the Terrorist Attacks on the United States. Washington, D.C.: Arab American Institute.

_____. 2000. Culture Polls. Ithaca, New York: Zogby International.

_____. 1995. Arab American Institute/Zogby Group Poll. October 26-30. Washington, DC: Arab American Institute.

_____. 1990. Arab America Today: A Demographic Profile of Arab Americans. Washington,   DC: Arab American Institute.

Index

Printed in the United States
94188LV00010B/1/A

9 781593 320065